ABUNDANT GRACE

Copyright © J. B. Adeyemi 2013

All rights reserved. No part of this book may be reproduced by any means whatsoever without prior permission of the author.

All scriptures are from New King James Version of the Bible unless otherwise stated.

Published by
GOSPEL PENTECOSTAL ASSEMBLY
(The Glorious Family)
NO 5/7 Olusola Street, Off Union Road,
Cement Bus Stop, Abeokuta expressway,
Dopemu, Lagos, Nigeria
P. O. Box 2328, Agege, Lagos
Tel. 08072888191
E-mail: johnsonadeyemi_rev@yahoo.com
Website:www.jbadeyemi.com
Twitter:@jbadeyemi
Facebook: www.facebook.com/jbadeyemi

CONTENTS

Dedication 3

Appreciation 4

Introduction 5

Chapter 1: **The Nature of Divine Grace** 8

Chapter 2: **The Dispensation of Grace** 20

Chapter 3: **Abundant Grace** 36

Chapter 4: **Salvation by Grace** 59

Chapter 5: **Sufficiency & Strengthening Grace** 76

Chapter 6: **Serving Grace** 91

Chapter 7: **Purpose of Grace in Service** 108

Chapter 8: **Standing Grace** 125

Chapter 9: **Falling from Grace** 140

Chapter 10: **Proper Attitude to Divine Grace** 151

Chapter 11: **Growing in Grace** 163

Chapter 12: **Evidences of Growing in Grace** 174

Chapter 13: **The Efficacy of Grace** 190

Bibliography 204

DEDICATION

This book is dedicated to the glory of The Godhead the Source, Planner and Giver of abundant grace, and to the grace of our God and the Lord Jesus Christ.

APPRECIATION

I wish to express my profound appreciation to my editor, proof-readers, my sons, and secretary who did the type-setting of this book.

I thank the ministers, Elders, Deacons, Deaconesses, Workers and entire members of Gospel Pentecostal Assembly for their steadfast love and support at all times.

I am highly indebted to my wife and children for their support, co-operation and understanding which added in no small way to my concentration and resourcefulness.

Finally, to God be the glory for testimonies and feedback received from some readers of my last book: TIME TO PREPARE FOR ETERNITY. The book is now on sale on the internet: amazon.com

I am trusting the Lord that readers of this book will not receive the grace of God in vain.

INTRODUCTION

Grace is God's mercy towards mankind even though we don't deserve it. It is the nature of God's character to exercise goodwill towards His creature. Grace is the gift of God by which He extends mercy, loving kindness and salvation to people. God's grace enables Him to confront human indifference and rebellion with His unlimited capacity to forgive and bless. God's grace began in the Garden of Eden with Adam and Eve, though they were punished for their sin and sent away from the garden, yet they were not forsaken. Salvation was provided through the seed of the woman.

Ultimately, it was the death of Jesus on the cross that enables sinners who repent to access God's forgiving and restorative grace which is described as the doctrine of justification by faith through grace (Rom. 3: 23,24).

God in the riches of His goodness gives grace in abundance to believers for several purposes; to help them maintain their salvation, to excel in every realm of life and to surmount obstacles. Paul describes this special grace as "abundant grace" (2 Cor. 4:15). "Abundance" means "more than sufficient" or "plentiful". God gives us His grace – freely, richly, and abundantly – depending on the areas and levels of our need for grace- sufficiency and strengthening grace; grace for service; standing grace by which we are kept from falling or failing; growing grace that enables us to progressively become like Christ and the grace that enables believers to accomplish God's purpose in our lives. Divine Grace is unlimited, supernatural and comprehensive in its essence, scope and transforming power. It is efficacious, as the word and the Atonement are; no one is beyond the reach and power of divine grace.

Great grace is needed where great work is to be accomplished. The more the level of our responsibility, the more should be the level of our grace. Great grace is needed for great exploits, great assignments and for great results. The apostles did not only receive "great power" they received "great grace as well. There must be a reasonable balance between power for ministry and grace for service (Acts 4:33).

While every believer has the same level of "saving grace", we all do not have the same level of grace for ministry or service. This book will enable the reader to find his level which may be the basic level of saving grace and how to stand in grace or receive grace for your own level in the ministry or service.

The book covers a wide range of theological themes on Grace profoundly, thoroughly, realistically and robustly. It clearly reflects the author's depth of knowledge and grasp of the Doctrine of Grace, biblically, theologically, 'dispensationally' and experientially.

Since we do not have the same level of gifting, calling or responsibilities, it is reasonable to expect different levels of grace for these assignments. This book will enable you to rediscover yourself as a Bible College Student or a prospective minister of God, a serving minister or a worker. For an unbeliever or a new convert, this book provides you a platform for steady and progressive growth. As babies desire the sincere milk of the word that you may grow thereby (1 Pet. 2:2). You need this book as your companion from conversion until the end of your assignment here on earth. The author demonstrates a unique and distinct style, which qualifies him to write on this theme as a competent theologian, a seasoned shepherd, a veteran Bible Teacher and a gifted and graceful expositor.

You can join us in GPA to rejoice in His "Abundant Grace". Christ who saves us from sin has also promised to preserve us to the utter-most (Heb. 7:25). Therefore, "Christ is our sufficiency" (2 Cor. 12:9).

Rev. J. B. Adeyemi
June 1, 2013.

CHAPTER 1

THE NATURE OF DIVINE GRACE

The word "grace" is used in a variety of ways, depending on the individual's focus or preference. This variety of usage is clearly presented in the English Dictionary, as follows:

Pleasing quality, attractiveness, charm...belonging to elegant proportions or ease and refinement of movement, action, expression, or manner, attractive feature, accomplishment of extra note(s), the bestowment of beauty and charm. Favour, benignant regard, or its manifestation, on part of superior... enjoy his favour or liking, unconditional goodwill as ground of concession, unmerited favour, Mercy, clemency, general pardon...[1]

Most of the usages present the objective aspects of grace; they reflect divine grace on the beneficiaries. Grace is reflected in forms of beauty, elegance, charm, attractive feature or refinement, which have been bestowed by God to the individual.

To Christians and theologians, "grace" is primarily an "unmerited favour" bestowed by God. It is a favour we do not deserve or merit, but given to us on the basis of the goodness and kindness of God.

According to Matthew Henry:

Grace is the free, undeserved goodness and favour of God to mankind[2]

---

1. The Concise English Dictionary, London: Oxford University Press, 1961, P. 532
2. A Quote in Encyclopedia of Christian Quotations, Hamshire: John Hunt Publishing Inc., 2000, P. 445

It is by this grace that we receive invaluable blessings or benefits (Psalm 103: 1-5) – not inherent in man – but bestowed by God. Thus, by this divine grace, we are freely pardoned, saved, justified, healed, delivered and used by God.

Grace and Mercy

Grace is sometimes used synonymously with "mercy"; though they both share a common source – God, and a common distinctive characteristic – "underserved" or "unmerited" – yet they are not exactly the same. Mercy is a product of divine "compassion", or "pity" while grace is more of divine "favour" or "kindness". Hence the phrase: "to temper justice with mercy". When someone who deserves to be punished, in accordance with divine justice is set free, we call it "mercy". And when a person who does not deserve something receives it, we call it "grace".

This is profoundly stated by an unknown author:

Grace is what God gives us when we don't deserve and mercy is when God doesn't give us what we do deserve.[3]

As sinners, we deserved death, in accordance with Divine justice. But, because of God's "mercy", death sentence has been waived; for Jesus has died in our stead, so that we might live. But the "freed" and "pardoned" sinner is "saved" and freely justified not because he deserves or merits it – but because of the grace of God.

---
3. Ibid; P. 442

For all have sinned, and come short of the glory of God; Being justified freely by his grace through the redemption that is in Christ Jesus.
(Rom. 3:23, 24)

Grace, mercy and peace are sometimes mentioned together in that order – especially in Paul's epistles (See: 1 Tim. 1:2; 2 Tim. 1:2; Tit. 1:4). Grace always comes before mercy; grace describes the attitude of God towards those who have sinned, while mercy describes His attitude to those in distress. Peace is the resulting experience in the heart of man. Grace and mercy are combined in the pardon and justification of a sinner, which results to peace with God and within one's heart: "Being justified by faith, we have peace with God" (Rom. 5:1).

Grace and Nature

The natural man is controlled by nature, which is weak and imperfect. But grace perfects nature; though it does not abolish it, but it refines and changes it positively. Human nature is corrupt, evil and has the propensity to act wickedly, against Divine law of righteousness. But the grace of God is supernatural, influencing the natural man to act well in conformity with God's righteousness.

Benard of Clairvaux said:

Simply to will comes from man's nature; to will wickedly comes from corrupt nature; to will well, from supernatural grace[4]

God's grace is stronger than nature; grace is

---
4. Ibid; P. 447

supernatural, while nature is natural. It has a superseding influence over nature. Thus, when this supernatural influences human nature, a change is inevitable. It makes a difference between natural and regenerated people. It is the supernatural influence which overshadows the natural.

Grace is so strong and efficacious that it can reach any vile or wicked soul. It can supernaturally change any corrupt nature, however bad it may seem to be.

John Owen wrote:

If grace doth not change human nature, I do not know what grace doth[5]

The fallen man still carries some trait of "animality", even the educated and elites, making the fallen man morally depraved.

Divine grace is so powerful that it can reach a man in the gutter and make a jewel out of him; it can change a criminal into a credible character, and can refine rough characters.

Nature, without grace, struggles under the weight of sin and its guilt. But grace mediates and helps us overcome what seems impossible to nature. Thus, to lose or to be deprived of grace is to live by the limitations and imperfections imposed by nature.

Grace is the "strengthening influence" that makes us "become" who we are; we are better than who we were, because of the grace bestowed on us. It was in this sense of "becoming", that Paul spoke, when he

---
5. Ibid; 445

said:

By the grace of God I am what I am: and His grace which was bestowed upon me was not in vain; but I laboured abundantly than they all: yet not I, but the grace of God which was with me. (1 Corinthians 15:10)

Grace possesses "transforming power"; it supernaturally transforms the character of individual, to whom it is divinely bestowed. Paul confessed that, in time past, he "persecuted the church of God" (1 Cor. 15:9); therefore, he was not worthy to be called an apostle. But grace changed him totally; he testified:

But whatever I am now, it is all because God poured out His special favour on me.
(1 Cor. 15:10 NLT)

John Newton shared Paul's experience, when he said:

I am not what I ought to be; I am not what I wish to be: I am not what I hope to be: but by the grace of God I am what I am[6]

When God's nature is imparted on human nature, we receive His grace to reflect His divine life through us. Thus, we can partake in His divine nature and overcome the world's corruption caused by human desires.

Whereby are given unto us exceeding great and

---
6. Ibid; 447

precious promises: that by these ye might be partakers of the divine nature, having escaped the corruption that is in the world through lust.
(Peter 1:4)

The fallen man still carries some trait of "animality", even those considered as "cultured" or educated. This explains the moral depravity of fallen and graceless humans. But divine grace is bestowed to help us "conform to the image" of Jesus Christ (Rom. 8:29).

The Biblical meaning of Grace

The original words used in the Bible describes "grace" as an "unmerited favour", an act of kindness or favour from a superior to the less privileged.

According to Paul, God's salvation or favour are not gained by human efforts or hard work; it is purely by His mercy.

In Romans 9:16, Paul declares:

So then it is not of him who wills, nor of him who runs, but of God who shows mercy.

A study of the words used in both the Old and New Testaments will give us a better understanding of the meaning and various usages of grace.

In the Old Testament

The Hebrew word used for "grace" in the Old Testament, is "chen"; it is a word derived from "chanan", which denotes to bend or stoop in kindness to an inferior, to favour, to move to favour, to be gracious, to have pity. While chanan is used for graciously (Gen. 33:6, 11), gracious (Gen. 43:29; Exd. 34:6; Job 33:24; Isa. 30:18, 19), chen is the word used for grace. It is used in the sense of graciousness, either for the subject for favour, kindness or the object as favour, grace, beauty, pleasant (Prov. 5:19), precious (Prov. 17:8), gracious (Prov. 11:16; Eccl. 10:12).

The Hebrew word is translated 'grace' thirty seven times and 'favour' twenty five times. Thus, grace and favour are used synonymously in the Old Testament; where there is grace, favour is bestowed.

It is used in reference to Divine grace or favour or human favour or both. But Divine grace opens the door to favour from humans to an inferior.

In relation to Divine grace bestowed, we are told:

But Noah found grace in the eyes of God.
(Genesis 6:8)

This "grace", from the Hebrew word 'chen', is obviously referring to the favour of God; not in the sense of becoming, but in the sense of God's act of kindness towards Noah.

In the New Living Translation, it reads:

But Noah found favour with the LORD.

The same word is used for Divine favour, in reference to Samuel.

And the child Samuel grew on, and was in favour both with God and also with men.
(1 Samuel 2:26)

The word is used as grace and favour from the king towards Esther.

And Esther obtained favour in the sight of all them that looked upon her...And the king loved Esther above all the women, and she obtained grace...in his sight more than all virgins...
(Esther 2:15, 17)

Again, we are told:

And it was so, when the king saw Esther the queen standing in the court, that she obtained favour in his sight...
(Esther 5:2)

The grace of God upon Joseph was evident to the people who showed favour towards him.

And Joseph found grace in his sight...But the LORD was with Joseph, and shewed him mercy and gave him favour in the sight of the keeper of the prison. (Genesis 39:4, 21)

As we can see, the same Hebrew word used for 'grace' in verse 4, is translated 'favour' in verse 21. The Scripture also reveals that Divine grace or favour supersedes human favour; human favour is the product of Divine grace, whom God bestows His favour will be received with favour by men.

In the New Testament

The Greek word for grace, charis, is used in a variety of ways, like it is used in the Old Testament. In the New Testament, however, its application to the redemptive purpose of God is more prominent. The word usually means an "unmerited favour", the gift we receive "freely" from God. The usual Greek word used for gift is charisma, which shares a common root with 'charis'. Thus, "gift" and "grace" are related in the sense that "gift" is freely given by the Sovereign will of God; the gift is given as an act of God's grace, not merited by the possessor. This way, it is a gift of grace, or a gift involving grace on the part of God, which is freely bestowed on sinners (Rom. 5:15, 16; 6:23; 11:29).

In 2 Corinthians 8:4, 'charis' is used for gift, instead of the usual Greek word 'charisma'.

Praying us with much entreaty that we would receive the gift...

The word implies 'grace', when applied in its context; this is suggested in verses 6, 7, where grace is used: "So he would also finish in you the same grace also" (verse 6); "See that ye abound in this grace also" (verse 7).

Generally, the Greek word for grace, 'charis', is used either in an objective sense or a subjective sense, as follows:

a. **Objective:** it refers to that which bestows or occasions pleasure, delight, or causes favourable regard: it is applied, e. g. to beauty, or gracefulness of person, Luke 2:40; act, 2 Cor. 8:6 or speech, Luke 4:22; Col. 4:6[7]

b. **Subjective:** it is used as follows: i) on the part of the bestower, the friendly disposition from which the kindly act proceeds, graciousness, loving-kindness, goodwill generally, e. g. Acts 7:10; especially with reference to Divine favour or grace, e. g. Acts 14:26...[8]

In this respect, 'grace' stresses the freeness and universality, its spontaneous character, when used in reference to God's redemptive mercy and the joy and pleasure which God designs for the recipient. In this way, it is clearly distinguished from debt (Rom. 6:4, 16), works (Rom. 11:6) and the law (John 1:17).

c. In another objective sense, the effects of grace, that is, the spiritual condition of those who have exercised grace, whether:
i) A state of grace, as in Rom. 5:2; 1 Pet. 5:12; 2 Pet. 3:18, or
ii) The evidence of its efficacy in practical realities, such as the deeds of grace, the "liberality" or "bounty" (from 'charis', in 1 Cor. 16:3; 2 Cor. 8:6, 19); in 2 Cor. 9:8, grace refers to the sum of earthly blessings, and the power and equipment for Christian service, as in Rom. 1:5; 12:6; 15:15; 1 Cor. 3:10; Gal. 2:9; Eph. 3:2, 7 etc.

---

7. See: W. E. Vine, Vine's Expository Dictionary of New Testament Words, Massachusetts: Hendrickson Publishers, (no date), P. 510
8. Ibid.

Grace and Favour

Like in the Old Testament, grace is used in the sense of favour in the New Testament. Thus, to find grace with, is to find favour with. The Greek word for grace is translated "favour" sixteen times. (See Luke 1:30; 2:52; Acts 2:47; 7:10, 46; 25:3). In Acts 2:47, we are told: the church was "having favour with all the people. And the Lord added to the church daily such as should be saved" (Acts 2:47).

Grace appears in this sense at the beginning and end of Pauline epistles, where Paul desired Divine grace for the people.

Grace to you and peace from God our Father and the Lord Jesus Christ. (1 Cor. 1:3)

The grace of our Lord Jesus be with you.
(1 Cor. 16:23)

Divine grace is said to be bestowed (1 Cor. 15:10; 2 Cor. 8:1), given (Eph. 3:8; 4:7) or received (2 Cor. 6:11; Gal. 2:9). Grace is received both from the Father (2 Cor. 1:12) and from the Son (Gal. 1:6) or from both (Rom. 5:15).

This is a positive testimony to the Divinity of Jesus Christ. This is clearly revealed in Paul's second letter to the Thessalonians:

That the name of our Lord Jesus Christ may be glorified in you, and ye in him, according to the grace of our God and the Lord Jesus Christ.
(2 Thessalonians 1:12)

The Apostle James exhorts Christians to be humble, so that they might be lifted up by God; for He gives "more grace" to the humble, but resists the proud.

But He gives more grace. Therefore He says: God resists the proud, But gives grace to the humble.
(James 4:6)

God will bestow "greater grace" to Christians who live and serve God in humility. Peter confirms James' exhortation in 1 Peter 5:5, where he said, "God resisteth the proud, but giveth grace to the humble".

CHAPTER 2

THE DISPENSATION OF GRACE

This present Age or Dispensation is also known as the Dispensation of Grace. This is established on John's statement in John 1:17.

For the law was given by Moses, but grace and truth came by Jesus.

First, John sets grace in contrast with law; grace follows and is superior to law. However, both are two aspects of God's nature in dealing with us. Moses emphasized God's law and justice, but Jesus came to highlight God's grace or mercy which results to forgiveness, love and kindness. Moses could give the law, but Christ came to fulfill the law (Matt. 5:17). The nature and will of God were revealed in the Law; but the nature and will of God are now revealed in Jesus Christ. Thus, we no longer live under the tables of the Law, but under grace which God has provided through Jesus Christ.

Paul spoke about the transition from law to grace; we are no longer under the law but under grace.
For sin shall not have dominion over you, for you are not under law but under grace. What then? Shall we sin because we are not under law but under grace? Certainly not! (Romans 6:14-15).

Paul also spoke about this period as "the Dispensation of Grace".

If indeed you have heard of the dispensation of grace of God which was given me for you (Ephesians 3:2)

A dispensation is defined as:
Distribution, dealing out; ordering; management; especially of the world by nature or Providence; special dealing of Providence with community or person; religious system prevalent at a period ...[9]

Paul used the Greek word Oikonomia for "dispensation" in Eph. 3:2, which denotes management of a household or of household affairs. Then, it is used to signify management or administration of the property of others. It is used by Paul of the "Dispensation of the Gospel" (1 Cor. 9:17) and the "Dispensation of Grace" (Eph. 3:2).

In Eph. 1:10, it is used of the arrangement or administration by God, by which "in the fullness of time" God will bring everything together under the authority of Christ.

That the dispensation of the fullness of the times He might gather together in one all things in Christ both which are in heaven and which are in earth – in Him. (Ephesians 1:10).

W.E. Vine defines a dispensation as "a mode of dealing" rather than "a period or epoch". He said:

A dispensation is not a period or epoch... but a model of dealing, an arrangement or an administration of affairs.[10]

---

9. The Concise Oxford Dictionary, London: Oxford University Press, 1961, P. 353

10. W. E. Vine, Vine's Expository Dictionary of New Testament Words, Massachusetts: Hendrickson, no date, P. 323.

In conformity with the Dictionary definition, as "special dealing of Providence with a community ... at a period", Dispensational Theologians view it both as a mode of dealing and a period. It is a period of time in which God deals with His people in accordance with His redemptive plan and purpose.

Each dispensation has its own features and period, designed by God. The next is an improvement upon the previous one, in progressive revelation.

According to Dispensational Theologians, there are seven dispensations, which are:
a.   INNOCENCE
b.   CONSCIENCE
c.   HUMAN GOVERNMENT
d.   PROMISE
e.   LAW
d.   CHURCH or GRACE
f.   KINGDOM AGE

Dispensations are periods of human history planned by God to fulfil His redemptive purpose. Dispensation is a historical sequence of divine administrations unfolding God's plan for mankind. The change in dispensation is not because God changes but mankind does and shifts from eternal purpose of God, hence the integration of divine conciliation to bring mankind close to Himself. The changes God incorporates into His plan are designed to attain His unchangeable purpose (Heb. 6:17, 18), to reveal His unchangeable glory, wisdom and power, under different conditions.

a.   **Dispensation of Innocence**
This first period is known as positive volition or perfection or innocence because of the absence of

sin in man. Mankind stayed within limits accorded him and had unfettered fellowship with God. Divine plan was for mankind to rule the earth forever under obedience to the divine rule.

The first couple (Adam and Eve) violated divine order by eating the forbidden fruit in flagrant disobedience to God's injunction, having fallen victim to Satan's grand deception. Consequently, they were expelled from the Garden of Eden which also ended the dispensation of innocence (Gen. 3:22-24).

b.   **Dispensation of Conscience**
After man committed sin of disobedience against God, his conscience gripped of his error, he tried to hide but there was no hiding place for him, his sin found him out. The marred conscience could no longer stay with the holy God because the holiness he shared with God was no more available to him. After the fall, the devil attacked the first seed of the woman, Cain, who killed his brother Abel, because God accepted his offering while Cain's offering was rejected (Gen. 4:24). Before the flood, apart from few exemptions which include Enoch and Noah, people were corrupt, desperately wicked and filled with violence (Gen. 6:5, 12, 13). Consequently, God decided to do away with the people in the days of Noah but Noah and his family found grace and survived the flood. God closed the second dispensation with judgment on earth when flood swept away and destroyed everything on earth.

c.   **Dispensation of human government**
After the flood, Noah presented sweet smelling sacrifice to God (Gen. 8:15-9:3) and God made a covenant with Noah and his seed, not to destroy mankind any more with water or flood (Gen. 8:21).

Under this dispensation God offered another opportunity to mankind to govern and populate the earth and to put to death anyone who would shed his fellow man's blood (Gen. 9:6). The people were united in language and mind up till the time they resolved to build the Tower of Babel – to build a city and a tower reaching heaven; to make a name for themselves; to be in a place so that they would not scatter. The people's plan and ambition ran counter to God's covenant with Adam (Gen. 1:28) and Noah (Gen 9:1) and constituted disobedience and rebellion against God. Consequently, God confused their language and the people scattered and this brought an end to the third dispensation (Gen. 11:6-9).

d.   **Dispensation of Promise**
The fourth dealing with the apostate race, known as dispensation of promise, started with Abraham's call who abandoned the worship of idols, believed God and answered the call (Gen. 12:1-3).The dispensation of promise, otherwise referred to as Abrahamic Covenant, contains individual promises, national promises to Israel and universal blessings to all nations (Gen. 15:1-5, 13, 14; 22:16-18; 2 Cor. 8:9; Gal. 3:13, 14). Jacob and his descendants came to settle in Egypt and domiciled there for 430 years (Gen. 46:1-6; Exd. 12:36-40). This dispensation came to a partial end when Moses received the law at Sinai.

e.   **Dispensation of Law**
The fifth dispensation commenced when God gave the two tables of the law to Moses at Sinai. For several years Israel had known other nations including Egypt where they grew up and knew only Egyptian ways of life. In order to fill this vacuum, God gave the law to His people so that they might

know the will and the way of the Almighty God. Eventually, the law was observed more in breach than in observance. The law merely condemned them. The Lord Jesus Christ came to save mankind from the curse of sin not by abrogating the law but by fulfilling the law. He died on the cross for our sin (John 3:16) and rose for our justification, thereby mankind who believes Him might become the righteousness of God (2 Cor. 5:21).

f.   **Dispensation of Grace**
The Dispensation of Grace, the sixth dispensation, which is viewed as the best, is superior to the Law. Moreover, in all the dispensations of the Old Testament, God spoke through human agents. But He now speaks directly to us through His Son, Jesus Christ.

God who at various times and in various ways spoke in time past to the fathers by the prophets, has in these last days spoken to us by His Son, whom He has appointed heir of all things, through whom also He made the worlds. (Hebrews 1:1-2).

The superiority of Grace over Old Testament Dispensations

All the pre-church dispensations were inferior to grace in many respects. The Law, for example, was imperfect, limited and incapable of procuring true holiness. But the grace of God makes holiness and victory over sin a possibility. The Law was designed to be temporary, until the coming of Jesus Christ, to usher in the dispensation of Grace.

For what the law could not do in that it was weak through the flesh, God did by sending His only Son in the likeness of sinful flesh, on account of sin: He condemned sin in the flesh.
(Romans 8:3)

The superiority of the present dispensation – of Grace – is described by Paul as "better". That is, in comparison with others, this Age of Grace is "better" or superior; it provides the following superior privileges:

a.) **Better Revelation**
The word translated 'better' comes from the Greek word "Kreisson", which derives its root from "Kratos" which means "strong" (which denotes power in activity and effect), serves as the comparative degree of "agathos" (good or fair). The word "Kreisson" translated "better" is especially characteristic of the Epistle to the Hebrews where it is used 12 times; it indicates what is (a) advantageous or useful, (1 Cor. 7:9,38;11:17; Heb. 11:40), where it is coupled with "mallon" translated more, and pollo "much, by far", "very far better"; (b)Excellent, (Heb 1:4; 6:9; 7:7,19,22; 8:6; 9:23; 10:34; 11;16,35).[11]

Revelation is God's communication to mankind concerning Himself, His moral standards, His plan of salvation and plan for end time. God has made Himself known to all people everywhere in the marvels of nature and in the human conscience which is able to distinguish right from wrong (Rom. 2:14-15).

---
11. See: Ibid., P. 124

In the past, under the five dispensations that preceded the dispensation of grace, God spoke to our ancestors many times and in many ways through the prophets. But in this age of grace, God speaks to us directly through His Son, Jesus Christ, in clear language.

Explaining the purpose of parables to His disciples, Jesus said: "To you it has been given to know the mysteries of the Kingdom of God, but to the rest it is given in parables, that seeing they may not see, and hearing they may not understand" (Luke 8:10). Christ reveals everything concerning the Kingdom to all believers, the children of the Kingdom, but hidden to sinners because of their unbelief (Matt. 11:25; 13:15).

Paul, writing on better revelation, God's superior revelation, said:

God who at various times and in various ways spoke in time past to the fathers by the prophets, has in these last days spoken to us by His Son, whom He has appointed heir to all things, through whom also He made the worlds; who being the brightness of His glory and the express image of His person, and upholding all things by the Word of His Power when He had by Himself purged our sins, sat down at the right hand of Majesty on high, having become so much better than the angels, as He has by inheritance obtained a more excellent name than they.
(Hebrews 1:1-4).

b.) **Better Hope**
Hope means confident expectation, to anticipate, look forward to. In the Bible the word "hope" stands for both the act of hoping (Rom. 4:18; 1 Cor. 9:10) and the hoped for (Col. 1:5; 1 pet. 1:30). Hope does not rise from individual's desire or wishes but from God who is Himself the believer's hope. Hope has to do with the unseen and the future (Rom. 8:24, 25).

"The hope of the Gospel", that is, the "hope" of the fulfillment of all the promises presented in the gospel (Col. 1:5; Rom. 5:2), is "very far better" than all those promised in the Old Testament.

For example, in his letter to the Hebrews, Paul provided the picture of Christ's superiority by comparing Jesus to Melchizedek. Christ's leadership was universal, His priesthood was not limited to a single country. The leadership of Christ is eternal, not temporary, therefore He gives better hope to believers.

Paul writes on the greatness of the new Priest:

And inasmuch as He was not made priest without an oath (for they have become priests without an oath but He an oath by Him who said to Him: "The Lord has sworn and he will not relent, You are a priest forever according to the order of Melchizedek), by no much more Jesus has become a surety of a better covenant. Also there were many priests, because they were prevented by death from continuing.
But He, because He continues forever, has an unchangeable priesthood. Therefore He is also able to save to the uttermost those who come

**to God through Him, since He always lives to make intercession for them.
For such a High Priest was fitting for us, who is holy, harmless, undefiled, separate from sinners, and has become higher than the heavens; who does not daily, as those high priests, to offer up sacrifices, first for His own sins and then for the people's, for this He did once for all when He offered up Himself. For the law appoints as his priests men who have weakness, but the word of the oath, which came after the law, appoints the Son who has been perfected forever**.
(Hebrews 7:20-28)

Believers in Christ must endure under trial as we await the coming of Jesus, "the anchor of our soul", in order to stay amidst the storms of life (Heb. 6:16,19); and "everyone that has this hope set on Christ purifies himself even as He is pure" (1 John 3:3).

c.)   **Better Testament**
Testament is a written document that provides for the disposition of one's personal property after death, a bequest. The word "testament" occurs only two times in NKJV (2 Cor. 3:14; Heb. 9:16-17), but 13 times in the Authorized Version. It is translated from the Greek noun diatheke, which primarily signifies a disposition of property, that is, a contract, a will. It is more translated "covenant". The word "testament" also refers to either of the two divisions of the Bible: The Old Testament and the New Testament or more accurately, the Old covenant and the New Covenant (2 Cor. 3:14). The New Covenant is a better one when compared with the Old Covenant, the Law of Moses. The New Covenant

replaced the Old Covenant because of the shortcomings of the latter (Heb. 8:7).

Paul writes: "By so much more Jesus has become a surety of a better covenant" (Heb. 7:22).

Christ became the guarantee that the benefits of the new covenant would be given to all men who meet the terms.

Paul also wrote:

But now He has obtained a more excellent ministry, inasmuch as He is also mediator of a better covenant, which was established on better promises. (Hebrews 8:6)

Jesus attained a more excellent ministry because of the better covenant based upon better promises (Heb. 8:6; 2 Cor. 3:6-18).

d.) **Better Promises**
Promise is a solemn pledge to perform or grant a specified thing. All Biblical promises are made by God to human beings to demonstrate that His nature is characterized chiefly by grace and faithfulness. Grace prompted God to promise a new land to the Israelites (Exd. 12:25). His faithfulness enabled Him to fulfill that promise, in spite of the nation's disobedience. Paul pointed out in Galatians 3:15-29, that God's faithfulness and grace are particularly evident in His promise to Abraham. Christians have a better promise eventually fulfilled in the work of Christ (Heb 8:6), and they should trust completely that God's promise of eternal life (Heb. 9:15) is secure.

e.) **Better Sacrifice**
Sacrifice offerings were brought daily or periodically to God in the Old Testament times by which people hoped to atone for their sins and restore fellowship with God. Mankind is separated from fellowship with God and unable to restore life-giving fellowship because of our sin (Rom. 5:12). The sentence of death hangs over us because we are identified with Adam's fall (Rom. 5:14), ultimately this will result in physical death and eternal suffering in hell. By divine provision, Jesus paid the penalty for our sin and restored our fellowship with God. This better sacrifice is the sacrificial offering of Jesus Christ (Hebrews 9:10).

Writing on the greatness of Jesus sacrifice, Paul said:

Therefore it was necessary that the copies of the things in the heavens should be purified with these, but the heavenly things themselves with better sacrifices than these.
(Hebrews 9:23)

Jesus offered a better sacrifice because He did not enter into earthly holy places to minister on our behalf but into heaven to represent us (Heb. 9:24).

f.) **Better Possessions**
The reference to better possession is the everlasting inheritance believers share with Christ, an incorruptible and undefiled inheritance, that fades not, reserved for us in heaven (1 Pet. 1:4).

Paul wrote:

For you had compassion on me in my chains, and joyfully accepted the plundering of your

goods, knowing that you have a better and an enduring possession for yourselves in heaven.
(Hebrews 10:34)

The heroes and heroines of faith died in faith, and although they did not receive the tangible fulfillment of God's promises, they did see it from a distance. Their journey could only see the invisible future for a better homeland, but as for the Christians we have a better hope, promises and inheritance.

Paul spoke concerning this, in these words:

And these all, having obtained a good report through faith, received not the promise: God having provided some better thing for us, that they without us should not be made perfect.
(Hebrews 11:39-40)

g.) **Better Country**
When God told Abraham to leave the comfort of his home in Haran, his relatives and all his possessions so that he might start afresh in another land (Gen. 12: 1-3), Abraham caught the vision of a new land and obeyed God. The faith and vision of Abraham, the friend of God, the father of the Hebrews, in his long walk with God "looked for a city that has foundations, whose builder and maker is God" (Heb. 11:10). He looked forward to the heavenly city, he believed there was such a city, he waited for it, he persevered, rejoicing in hope, that in God's time and way he should be brought safely to it.

The heroes and heroines of faith looked forward to a better country and God is not ashamed to be their God, who is also the God of all believers. The gracious and great reward of their faith is by building a city for them.

Paul wrote:

Now they desired a better, that is, a heavenly country. Therefore God is not ashamed to be called their God, for He has prepared a city for them.
(Hebrews 11:16).

The heavenly country is better than any on this earth; it is better situated, better stored with anything that is good; better secured from everything that is evil and everything in it is better than the best in this world. Therefore, we should persevere, endure all inconveniences and close our eyes to all distractions and cleanse ourselves from all filthiness of the flesh and spirit perfecting holiness in the fear of God. (2 Cor. 7:1).

h.) **Better Resurrection**
The dead children of the Zarephath woman (1 Kings 17: 23) and the Shunamite woman (2 Kgs. 4:36) were restored to life after the prayers of Elijah and Elisha respectively. Christ had compassion on the son of the widow of Nain and restored him back to life (Luke 7:12). He also raised Lazarus from the grave (John 11:41-44). But all of them were subjected to natural death.

Many of the apostles were persecuted and killed for their faith but rejoiced for suffering for Christ because they looked forward to a better resurrection because Jesus is the resurrection and the life (John 11:25, 26). Paul writes: "If in this life only we have hope in Christ, we are of all men the most pitiable" (1 Cor.15:19).

Paul wrote:

Women received their dead raised to life again. Others were tortured, not accepting deliverance, that they might obtain a better resurrection.
(Hebrews 11:35)

The heroes and heroines of faith and believers in Christ are looking forward to a better resurrection.

i.) **Better things are provided**
God has provided good things for the world through His Son, Jesus Christ, who died for our sin and rose for our justification. This is the greatest gift ever given by God to mankind. Before His ascension, Jesus assured believers that He was going to the Father in heaven to prepare mansions for believers and promised to send the Holy Spirit to guide, lead, motivate and remind believers of all things He had taught us (John 14:26;15:26).

Christ had made provisions for all we ever need to survive the perils and tribulations in the world (2 Timo. 3:1; John 16:33). He is our Provider and Protector, there is no cause to fret about our personal needs and survival in the perilous world (Matt. 6:31-34; Phil 4:6,19).

What God has prepared for believers are enormous and beyond material things. Paul writes: "But it is written Eye has not seen, nor ear heard, nor have entered into the heart of man, the things which God has prepared for those who love Him. But has revealed them to us through His Spirit. For the spirit searches all things, yes, the deep things of God" (1 Cor. 2:9,10).

Paul also wrote:

God having provided something better for us, that they should not be made perfect apart from us.
                                             (Hebrews 11:40)

Since God has provided better things for the believers, He expects good things from us – holiness, integrity and godliness - because to whom much is given much is expected.

The blood of Jesus speaks "better things" than the blood of Abel.

Made perfect to Jesus the Mediator of the new covenant, and to the blood of sprinkling that speaks better things than that of Abel.
                                             (Hebrews 12:24)

There are several other great privileges and benefits we receive through grace, which the saints in the Old Testament did not have. One of these is the individual's personal relationship with God. Every true Christian can come directly to the throne of God or the "Mercy Seat" for divine help.

Paul writes:

Let us therefore come boldly to the throne of grace that we may obtain mercy and find grace to help in time of need
                                             (Hebrews 4:16).

CHAPTER 3

ABUNDANT GRACE

God is infinitely rich in everything, because He created everything, and possesses everything, He is infinitely "rich in mercy" (Eph. 2:4; 1 Pet1:3).

Paul speaks of the "riches of grace" which God possesses and is exercised towards His children. He speaks of "the riches of His goodness" (Rom 2:4: see also Exodus 34:6), "the riches of His glory", that is, of its manifestation in grace towards believers (Rom. 9:23; Eph. 3:15) and "the riches of His grace".

In whom we have redemption through His blood, and the forgiveness of sins, according to the riches of His grace.
(Ephesians 1:7)

Paul writes again:

...that in the ages to come He might show the exceeding riches of His grace in His kindness toward us in Christ Jesus.
(Ephesians 2:7)

After Moses shattered the first set of stone commandments, the Lord directed him to chisel out some replacement. Moses again went up to Mount Sinai with the two tablets of stone and the Lord passed before him and proclaimed:

The Lord, the Lord God, merciful and gracious, longsuffering, and abounding in goodness and truth.
(Exodus 34:6)

Because God possesses these "riches" in infinite quantum, He is able to supply all our needs – including grace-according to His inexhaustible storehouse in glory.

And my God shall supply all your need according to His riches in glory by Christ Jesus
(Philippians 4:19)

Moreover, God is able to make all grace abound, so that we can always have everything we need and plenty left over to share with others.

And God is able to make all grace abound toward you, that you, always having all sufficiency in all things, may have an abundance for every good work.
(2 Corinthians 9:8)

Abundant Grace

God gives grace in abundance to believers for several purposes; to help them maintain their salvation, to excel in every realm of life and to surmount obstacles.

Paul describes this special grace as "abundant grace":

For all things are for your sakes, that the abundant grace might through the thanksgiving of many redound to the glory of God.
(2 Corinthians 4:15)

"Abundant" means "more than sufficient" or "plentiful". God gives us His grace-freely, richly, and abundantly- depending on the areas and levels of our need for grace. Great grace is needed where great work is to be accomplished. The more the level of our responsibility, the more should be the level of our grace.

Great grace is needed for great exploits, great assignment and for great results. It is presumptuous and, indeed, misleading, to aspire for great gifts or great anointing without grace commensurate with our aspirations.

The apostles did not only receive "great power", they received "great grace" as well. There must be a reasonable balance between power for ministry and grace for service.

And with great power the apostles gave witness to the resurrection of the Lord Jesus. And great grace was upon them all.
(Acts 4:33)

In 2 Cor. 4:15, Paul used the Greek word "Pleonazo", for abundant, which means to be more, greater in quantity, to super abound. The word is used of grace in Rom. 6:1 and 2 Cor. 3:15. The grace is also described as surpassing, exceeding, increasing and more. These descriptions are used for grace as follows:

a. **Abundant Grace**
Abundant means in large quantities; more than enough. The Old Testament or covenant of legal ordinances is like a veil, it blinds, hardens and condemns the Judaisers (the believers in the Law of Moses) because the law condemns. The veil on Moses' face, referred to by Paul in 2 Cor. 3:14, 15, is typical. The veil illustrates the fading of the system

and the veiling of the people's minds because of their pride, hardness of heart and unbelief. They remained hardened without understanding because they refused to come to Christ. But whenever someone realizes that the Law is done away in Christ, and turns to Him in repentance, the veil will be taken away and will no longer cover their hearts.

The Word of God declares, "but as many as received Him, gave He power to become the sons of God, even to them who believe His name" (John 1:12). This is the abundant grace bestowed on all believers in Christ because their veil are taken away and thereby they have direct access to Jesus Christ.

Paul writes:

But even to this day, when Moses is read, a veil lies on their hearts nevertheless when one turns to the Lord, the veil is taken away.
(2 Corinthians 3:15-16.)

b. **Exceeding Grace**

To exceed means to go beyond the limit or measure of. Exceeding grace is an extraordinarily great, huge, enormous, excessive or exceptional grace. The conversion and salvation of man and great sinners, no matter how wicked they were, are owing to the grace of Christ, his exceedingly abundant grace.

Paul wrote:

And the grace of our Lord was exceedingly abundant, with faith and love which are in Christ Jesus.
(1 Timothy 1:14)

In his epistle to the Corinthians, in chapter 9, Paul was not inclined in pressing the church to the duty of charity but proceeded to give directions about the acceptable way and manner of performing it bountifully and freely and encouraged them to give while reminding them; "and their prayer for you who long for you because of the exceeding grace of God to you" (2 Cor. 9:14).

c. **More Grace**

'More', when used as a determiner means extra; further or supplementary.

In chapter 4 of the epistle of James, the writer traced some cause of contention in the church to the emotions of people which revealed selfish goals: lust, envy, quarreling and fighting which often led to hostilities. James warned that God resists the proud- those who resist the truths of God and thus they resist the providence of God. He has admonished us to resist pride in our hearts if we would not have God resist us. But the honour and help God gives to the humble is grace as opposed to disgrace which goes to the proud. God's grace enables one to be humble and thereby He will give other graces, in other words, more grace.

But He gives more grace. Therefore He says: "God resists the proud, but gives more grace to the humble.
(James 4:6).

Wherever God gives true grace, He will give more; for to everyone who has, more will be given, and he will have abundance; but from him who does not have, even what he has will be taken away". (Matthew 25:29)

d. **Greater Grace**
Great means big, large, of high degree, of magnitude, beyond the ordinary, while greater means elevated in power, rank, station. Despite the persecution from the Sanhedrin the apostles went on in their work with great vigour and success. The doctrine they preached according to the record in Acts 4:33 was resurrection of Christ, to confirm the privileges and comforts of the new Christian religion. The miracle which they wrought confirmed the doctrine with work of great power, they gave witness to the resurrection of Christ and God Himself bearing witness too.

And with great power the apostles gave witness to the resurrection of the Lord Jesus. And great grace was upon them all.
(Acts 4:33)

The apostles encountered divine favour in all their performances and great grace was upon them all; not only all the apostles, but all the believers. In other words, Christ poured abundant grace-very extra-ordinary grace-upon them which qualified them for great services by enduing them with great power.

e. **Increasing Grace**
Something is said to be increasing when it is expanding, stepping up, developing or advancing.

In his prayer for the Thessalonian church in 3:12, Paul said:

And may the Lord make you increase and abound in love to one another and to all just as we do to you.

Mutual love is required of all Christians for the purpose of promoting charitable disposition of the mind and due concern for the welfare of one another and for all men. Love is of God, and is the fulfilling of the gospel as well as of the law.

Though Timothy brought good news to Apostle Paul concerning the Thessalonian church, but something (charity) was missing, so Paul prayed for them to increase and abound in charity. We have reason to desire to grow in every grace as Christians but the way to obtain it is by prayer.

Different levels of Grace

While every believer has the same level of "saving grace", we all do not have the same level of grace for ministry or service.

Since we do not all have the same level of gifting, callings or responsibilities, it is reasonable to expect different levels of grace for these assignments.

Basically, like spiritual gifts, our levels of favour depends primarily on the sovereign will of God (1 Cor 12:11). However, there are other factors which determine the difference in the level of grace. These include:

a. **The level of gifting**
The Greek word for 'gift' is 'charisma'. 'Charis' as we have seen, means grace and 'mah' means thing. Therefore, the New Testament word translated 'gift'

really means 'thing of grace'. When the scriptures talk about spiritual gifts, they are talking about an expression or manifestation of the grace of God in our lives. When we are saved by grace, we become eligible for the gifts and call of God. The seed of what God wants us to be will often be planted in us at conversion. God is not a respecter of persons when He distributes the gifts of the Holy Spirit (Heb. 2:4).

Paul wrote:

Having then gifts differing according to the grace that is given to us, let us use them: if prophecy, let us prophesy in proportion to our faith.
(Romans 12:6)

Paul also wrote:

But to each one of us grace was given according to the measure of Christ's gift.
(Ephesians 4:7)

b. **The level of ministry**
The Greek word diakonos is translated 'minister' in Mark 10:43; Rom 13:4; 15:8; Colo. 1:7 etc., while diakonia is translated "the office and work of a "diakonos". There are various aspects of ministering such as apostolic ministry (Acts 1:17, 25, 6:4); the service of believers (Acts 6:1); "to do serve" (to minster), the work of the gospel in general (2 Cor. 3:9), "of righteousness" (2 Cor. 5:9) "of reconciliation" (2 Cor. 5:18). The general "ministry" of a servant of the Lord is preaching and teaching (Acts 20:24, 2 Cor 4:1; 6:3).

In reality all believers are ministers, but it is the responsibility of Pastor-teacher to equip the saints so that they can minister to one another (Eph. 4:11-12).

Our selfless service should be rendered through our spiritual gifts, which are given by God to the saints in order that they might minister to one another (1 Pet. 4:10)

The gifts consist of both spiritual and practical gifts (1Cor. 12:28). They are distributed to members of the church according to their abilities and level of ministry. Paul, writing to the church in Rome, said: "so as much as is in me, I am ready to preach the gospel to you who are in Rome" (Rom. 1:15).

Nevertheless, brethren, I have written more boldly to you on some points, as reminding you, because of the grace given to me by God.
(Romans 15:15)

Paul again wrote:

According to the grace of God which was given to me, as a wise master builder, I have laid the foundation, another builds on it. But let each one take heed how he builds on it.
(1 Corinthians 3:10)

c. **Type of Calling**
Every saint is assigned the sphere of responsibility best suited to his/her temperament and given the grace (gifts) to enable him/her to accomplish the calling of God for his/her life individually or collectively, working conjunctively with others.

For example, when the apostles perceived the calling of God upon Paul and Barnabas as missionaries to the Gentiles and they (the apostles) to the Jews, they gave the hand of fellowship to the missionaries.

Paul wrote:

And when James, Cephas, and John, who seemed to be pillars, perceived the grace that had been given me, they gave me and Barnabas the right hand of fellowship, that we should go to the Gentiles and they to the circumcised.
(Galatians 2:9)

Paul wrote again:

Of which I became a minister according to the gift of grace of God given to me by the effective working of His Power.
(Ephesians 3:7)

d. **Level of Responsibility**

Whatever position or office of responsibility we attain in life or the ministry is only attributable to divine grace. When Paul looked back to the era of his being a persecutor of the church, he traced his marvelous conversion and labours as an apostle to the grace of God.

But by the grace of God I am what I am, and His grace toward me was not in vain; but I laboured more abundantly than they all, yet not I, but by the grace of God which was with me.
(1 Corinthians 15:10)

This is a reminder to all Christians that we are what we are, not by our hard work or wisdom, but by the grace of God. The repetition of the word 'grace' by Paul means God must take the glory, honour and dominion for all our accomplishments because without Him we can do nothing. And to whom much is given much will be required (Luke 12:48).

e. **The degree of its needs**
Christ died and took our sin upon Himself and imputed His righteousness on us and this made it appear as if we have never committed sin (2 Cor. 5:21). The more sin that resided in us before our conversion, the more abundant grace became to remit so much corruption. In other words, the greater the strength of our enemy, satan, the greater the honour and power of the conqueror, Jesus Christ, our Saviour. Thus, we become "more than conquerors" through Christ who strengthens us.

Shall we then take encouragement to sin with so much impunity because the more sin we commit, the more grace of God will magnify our pardon? No. it is an abuse, and far from us to have such thought. Apostle Paul tried to disabuse the minds of believers in Romans 5:20; 6:1-2 that the doctrine of justification that pardons and blots out our sin, regardless of its enormity and consequences, is not a license to go back to sin:

Moreover the law entered that the offence might abound. But where sin abounded, grace abounded much more.
(Romans 5:20)

What shall we say then? Shall we continue in sin that grace may abound? Certainly not! How shall we who died to sin live longer in it?
(Romans 6:1-2)

The Effects of Abundant Grace

A Christian who is given "more grace" or "abundant grace" will achieve more results or reflect abundant blessings. More divine grace and accomplishments will accrue to him. Conversely to whom much is given much will be desired.

The effects of abundant grace include:

a. **Abundant results**
Abundant means more than enough or in large quantities while abundant results means, profound success. It is God's prerogative to say; "I am that I am". It is our privilege to be able to say: "By God's grace we are what we are", as Paul declared in 1 Cor. 15:10.

But by the grace of God, I am what I am, and His grace toward me was not in vain: but I labourd more abundantly than they all, yet, not I, but the grace of God which was me.
(1 Corinthians 15:10)

We are nothing but what God's grace made us. All that is good in us is a stream from His fountain. Paul was conscious of his diligence, service and zeal but was humble and responsible enough to attribute his achievements to the grace of God.

There is an indwelling power (Holy Spirit) in the believer that propels him to do good works because "we are His workmanship created in Christ Jesus for good works" (Eph. 2:10).

As we have the grace of God bestowed on us, we should take care that it be not in vain. We should cherish it, use it to benefit His kingdom and labour with so much heart and so much success because we are debtors to divine grace.

b. **Abundant Joy**

When we talk of abundant joy, we are talking of unquantifiable joy, unspeakable joy full of glory of God. It is joy that flows from the throne of God, into human's heart, rich, and incomparable. Joy does not come from abundance of possession or wealth but flows from a feeling of fulfillment, having done the perfect will of God.

It was in this spirit, Paul wrote to the Corinthian church, in 2 Corinthians chapter 8, exhorting and directing them about a particular work of charity- to relieve the necessities of the poor saints at Jerusalem and in Judea, according to the example of the churches in Macedonia (Rom 15:26). The Christians in these parts met with ill treatment which had reduced them to deep poverty, yet as they had abundant of Joy in the midst of tribulation, they abounded in their liberality, they gave out of little, trusting in God to provide for them and make it up to them.

That a great trial of affliction the abundant of their joy and their deep poverty abound in the riches of their liberality.
                              (2 Corinthians 8:2)

Speaking of man's wickedness and God's loving kindness and perfection, who is the fountain of joy, David wrote:

How precious is Your loving kindness, O God! Therefore the children of men put their trust under the shadow of Your Wings. They are abundantly satisfied with the fullness of Your house, and You give them drink from the river of Your pleasures.
(Psalm 36:7-8)

c.   **Abundant Life**
Christ is the door and true shepherd, and not as the thief, not as those who came not in by the door. The mischievous design of the thief is to steal, kill and destroy spiritually for the heresies and false doctrines they preach and teach. The flock of Christ they could not influence, they persecute and kill.

The gracious plan of the shepherd is to give life to the sheep. Jesus Christ came to give life into the flock (the church). Jesus came to vindicate the truth, redress grievances and to seek His flocks that were lost. Jesus came to give life to believers; life includes all good things, just as life is restored to a pardoned criminal who had been condemned to death or to a sick man cured of a terminal disease.

This is the picture of Christ painted by John in John 10:

The thief does not come except to steal, and to kill and to destroy, I have come that they may have life, and that they may have it more abundantly.
(John 10:10)

Christ came to restore life to believers so that we might have a life more abundant than that which was lost and forfeited by sin, more abundant than that which was promised by the Law of Moses and more abundant than that which we can think or ask.

Abundant life is rich, full and overflowing; it is a fruit of abundant grace given by God, through Christ. The life we live in Christ is on a higher plane because of Christ's overflowing forgiveness, love and guidance. It is not limited to this world; it is eternal, though it begins immediately.

d. **Abundant Service**
Paul was forced to defend his ministry when it appeared he had lost his credibility in the eyes of the Corinthians. He had to enumerate his sufferings and abundant service rendered but he recognized that it was not by his power but by the abundant grace bestowed to him by the Lord.

Are they ministers of Christ? – I speak as a fool-I am more: in labours, more abundant, in stripes above measure, in prisons more frequently, in deaths, often.
(2 Corinthians 11:23)

e. **Abundant Power**
Paul, a man of passion, counseled the Ephesians church to be passionate about life and love it because passion is the first step to achievement. He prayed passionately that they comprehend the love of God (Eph. 3:14, 18), experience the love of Christ, and be filled with God (Eph. 3:19).

Paul declares:

Now to Him who is able to do exceedingly abundantly above all that we ask or think

according to the power that works in us.
(Ephesians 3:20)

f.   **Abundant Blessings**

Christians are always reminded to invest resources like farmers who sow seed and during harvest they reap exceedingly above what they sow. In the same token, as a Christian, it is what you sow that determines what you will reap (Gal. 6:7):

He who sows sparingly will also reap sparingly and he who sows bountifully will also reap bountifully.
(2 Corinthians 9:6).

On the basis of this law of sowing and reaping which brings abundant blessings, Paul admonished the Corinthians of the grace of God which is a guarantee of their sufficiency in all things.

And God is able to make all grace abound toward you, that you always having all sufficiency in all things, may have an abundance for every good work
(1 Corinthians 9:8)

After the revival and the reconciliation of the children of Israel with God during the ministry of Elijah, God put an end to the three and a half years of drought.

Then Elijah said to Ahab, go up, eat and drink; for there is the sound of abundance of rain
(1 Kings 18:41)

If you reconcile to God today by confessing your sin and forsaking same, He will forgive you and put an end to drought in your life, you will experience abundance of blessings. You will say like the Psalmist:

"You prepare a table before me in the presence of my enemies; You anoint my head with oil; my cup runs over (over flowing blessings).
(Psalm 23:5).

Moreover, God's abundant blessing makes a person rich and adds no sorrow with it (Prov. 10:22).

g. **Abundant Revelation**
Revelation means disclosure, exposure, uncovering, divulgence; biblically, it is God's communication concerning Himself, His moral standard and His plan of salvation. Revelation of John, the last book of the Bible, is also known as the Apocalypses; the title of the book in the original Greek, means 'unveiling' or 'disclosure' of hidden things known to God.

A lot of hidden things were revealed to Paul by God because he was highly favoured with spiritual gifts. This is what he referred to as abundance of revelations in 2 Corinthians 12:7.

And lest I should be exalted above measure by the abundance of revelations, a thorn in the flesh was given to me, a messenger of satan to buffet me, less I be exalted above measure.
(2 Corinthians 12:7)

The apostle was pained with a thorn in the flesh to check mate any feeling of arrogance or pride having been singularly endowed with abundance of revelations. Therefore, we are sometimes tempted that we may learn to pray and meditate on the word of God only to encounter new revelations.

Also God made abundance of revelation through Abraham. When God made promise to Abraham He backed it with an oath and He kept His promise. The promises of God are all founded in His eternal counsel which is immutable. The promise of blessedness which God made to believers is not rash but founded in His eternal purpose. We only have to wait with patience, like our father Abraham, to receive it.

Thus God determining to show more abundantly to the heirs of promise the immutability of His counsel; confirmed it by an oath. (Hebrews 6:17)

As God confirmed His good faith by using His name, Christians should make their words as good as a bond to personify both integrity and trustworthiness.

h. **Abundant Supplies**
When something is abundant it means it is more than enough. God supplies our needs in many supernatural ways, which are more than enough. While the disciples of Jesus were still debating the possibility of getting money and where to purchase enough food to feed a crowd of 5,000 men and numerous women and children, Christ already knew what He wanted to do. Eventually He fed the crowd from the five loaves of bread and two fish He collected from a boy and there were twelve baskets left-over.

Paul prayed for abundant supplies for the Philippian church who remembered to minister to Paul's need from time to time.

And with His abundant wealth through Christ Jesus, my God will supply all your needs.
(Philippians 4:19)

God has a limitless and inexhaustible resources from which to supply all the needs of His children. The Psalmist says in Psalm 23:

He sets a table before me, in the presence of my enemies... my cup is full and running over.

If you want to experience abundant supplies from His abundant wealth you should be ready to "give and it shall be given to you…" (Luke 6:38). What God gives in return is called abundant supplies because it is in multiples of yours.

Through the Psalmist there is divine promise of abundant provision:

I will abundantly bless her provision; I will satisfy her poor with bread.
                              (Psalm 132:15)

I.   **Abundant Entrance**
In his second epistle, Peter emphasized the need for Christians to experience fruitful growth in the faith. It is a process which we must go through and he went ahead to list eight characteristics of the process which include; faith, virtue, knowledge, self-control; perseverance, Godliness, brotherly kindness and love. He concluded that if we do all these things we will never stumble because they will provide great access for our entry into the kingdom of God.

For so an entrance will be supplied to you abundantly into the everlasting kingdom of our Lord and saviour Jesus Christ.
(2 Peter 1:11)

In Malachi 3:10, God promised to open the windows of heaven and pour His blessings upon all His obedient children that there will not be room enough to receive it. The doors or windows of blessings and opportunities are always locked against recalcitrant Christians.

The master key to door of prosperity is in the hand of God. When He opens, no one can shut, and when He shuts, no one can open (Isa. 22:22; Rev. 3:7-9). Repent from your sins and abundant entrance to blessings will be opened to you.

j. **Abundant Peace**
Peace means truce, pacification, conciliation, stillness, serenity, harmony. The word also signifies freedom from fear, anxiety and war. The Hebrew word for "peace", which is "Shalom", also means wellness, favour, wealth or favour. Great peace (Psalm 119:165), perfect peace (Isa. 26:3) or abundant peace (Jer. 33:6), is the desire of every man; it is the only source of true and lasting peace. The United Nations effort to ensure peace in the world has been a total failure. Only the Lord, "The Prince of Peace" (Isa. 9:6) can promise and give a lasting peace.

God has promised to keep in perfect peace those whose mind is stayed on Him (Isa. 26:3).

Speaking through the Psalmist, God says only the righteous will inherit the earth and enjoy abundant peace.

But the meek shall inherit the earth, and shall delight themselves in the abundance of peace.
(Psalm 37:11)

The Psalmist also writes:

In the His days the righteous shall flourish, and abundance of peace, until the moon shall be no more.
(Psalm 72:7)

k. **Abundant Pardon**
To pardon means to acquit, free, release, reprieve; a condemned criminal granted reprieve enjoys abundant pardon because he returns home a free man instead of being hanged.

This is the penalty Jesus paid for all sinners when He was nailed to the cross for the sins He never committed (John 3:16; Rom. 3:23). For every sinner that repents, abundant pardon awaits him. This repentant sinner is declared righteous by God, because Jesus has taken away his unrighteousness (2 Cor. 5:21).

Isaiah wrote:

Let the wicked forsake his way, and the unrighteous man his thoughts, let him return to the Lord, and He will have mercy on him; and to our God, for He will abundantly pardon.
(Isaiah 55:7)

I.   **Abundant Success**

Success means victory, triumph, favourable outcome or positive result. Abundant success means more than enough triumph or positive result.

God is the author of victory, triumph and breakthrough beyond the imagination of man.

Paul counseled the church to abound in purity more and more in the Lord in order to encounter abundant success

Finally then, brethren, we urge and exhort in the Lord Jesus that you should abound more, just as you received from us how you ought to walk and to please God.
(1 Thessalonians 4:1)

Job also emphasized the need to live righteously with clean hands in order to be empowered for victory and success.

Yet the righteous will hold to his way, and he who has clean hands will be stronger and stronger.
(Job 17:9)

The Psalmist in Psalm 1 compared the way of the righteous and the end of the ungodly and concluded on the righteous:

He shall be like a tree planted by the rivers of water, that brings forth its fruit in its season whose leaf also shall not whither, and whatever he does shall prosper.
(Psalm 1:3)

The Psalmist, writing on the blessedness of dwelling in the house of God, said:

They go from strength to strength, each one appears before God in Zion.
(Psalm. 84:7)

The Psalmist also wrote:

The righteous shall flourish like a Palm tree, he shall grow like a Cedar in Lebanon.
(Psalm 92:12)

Solomon wrote:

But the path of the just is like the shining sun, that shines ever brighter unto perfect day.
(Proverbs 4:18)

CHAPTER 4

SALVATION BY GRACE

Salvation is a Divine work, which we receive by faith in the redemptive work of Jesus Christ. It is purely by grace and, as such, it is entirely undeserved; it is not based on merit or received by human effort but by God's grace alone. Because salvation is directly linked with divine grace and brought to us by God's grace, the phrase, "saving grace" is used for the grace that brings salvation to sinful humanity.

Paul speaks about this "saving grace" in his epistle to Titus:

For the grace of God that bringeth salvation hath appeared to all men. Teaching us that, denying ungodliness and worldly lusts, we should live soberly, righteously, and godly, in this present world.

(Titus 2:11, 12 KJV)

The above scripture reveals three fundamental theological facts about saving grace.

Firstly, God's plan of salvation for sinful humanity is brought to us by the grace of God. Grace is the Divine instrument, the "carrier", the channel by which salvation is conveyed by God to men. Thus, without grace, no one will receive salvation; all men will be eternally lost, without grace.

Secondly, we are told that this grace has "appeared"- that is, the graciousness of God in the scheme of redemption has "appeared" or "hath been made to appear". Paul used the Greek word, "epiphaino" for "appear" in Titus 2:11, which denotes, to become visible, to give light, to become known.

In the New Living Translation, it is translated, "has been revealed". The word is used in an active voice with the meaning "to give light" (Luke 1:19), a reference to Jesus Christ quoted from the messianic prophecy of Isaiah (Isa. 9:2). It is also used of heavenly bodies, e.g, the sun and stars in Acts 27:20 and metaphorically of spiritual things: the grace of God (Tit. 2:11) and "the kindness and love of God our Saviour toward man..." (Tit. 3:4). The mystery of this "grace" had been kept hidden in the counsel of God for ages, in all the pre-church dispensations (see. Eph. 3: 3-5, 9; Col. 1:26). But it has been "made manifest by the appearing of our Saviour Jesus Christ" (2 Tim. 1:9-10). The grace of God has now been embodied in Christ; the "grace of God" rested manifestly, increasingly and fully in Him (Luke 2:40, 52); He is the Arm of God's salvation revealed (Isa. 53:1), the "Sun of Righteousness" (Mal. 4:2), the Light of the world (John 9:5; 12:46) and the Word that became flesh (John 1:14). Hence this Dispensation of grace (see: John 1:17; Eph. 3:2) and the Gospel is the gospel of the grace of God (Acts 20:32).

Thirdly, this saving grace is for "all men", it has "appeared to all men" (Tit. 2:11). God's free gift of salvation is for all men.

For God so loved the world that He gave His only begotten Son, that whoever believes in Him should not perish but have everlasting life. For God did not send His son into the world to condemn the world, but that the world through Him might be saved. (John 3:16, 17)

The purpose of God on the scheme of redemption is that all men should be saved. He is "not willing that any should perish, but that all should come to repentance" (2 Pet. 3:9).

As a gracious, loving and merciful God, He has no pleasure in the death of a sinner or the destruction of any soul (Ezek. 18:23, 32; 33:11).

While it is obvious that not "all men" will be saved; that not every soul will believe and receive saving grace provided through Christ (see Matt. 22:1-9; Isa. 65:12; John 5:40; Rom. 10:21), we have positive and imperative responsibilities towards "all men", in regard to the salvation of their souls. These include:

a. **To pray for all men**
The scripture emphasizes the importance of prayer in the life of Christians, hence the injunction to "pray without ceasing" (1 Thess. 5:17). Paul also gave prominence to the injunction that prayer be made for leaders and all men especially for magistrates and kings (1 Timo 2:1-4). Praying for our leaders and all men results in an atmosphere conducive to the spreading of the gospel.

b. **To preach to every creature**
The Divine mandate to all Christians otherwise called the Great Commission is to preach and teach the good news and make disciples of all nations, starting from the corner where we are (Matt. 28:19,20).

Writing to Timothy on the same subject, Paul charged Timothy on three priorities: (a) Preach the word; (b) do the work and (c) run the race (2 Timo. 4:1-8).

Before Jesus departed this world, He gathered His disciples and issued a final command. He told them to go and preach the gospel to every creature on earth (Mark 16:15-16). Just as He came to seek and save the lost, they were to continue the ministry and fulfill it. As Christ reproduced Himself in the disciples He mandated them to reproduce themselves. This is the transferable concept of reproduction Jesus passed to every believer.

c.   **To warn every man**
Warning, as used by Paul in is Col. 1:28, 29, is connected with repentance, refers to one's conduct, and it is addressed primarily to the heart. Everyman is included, without distinction of Jews or Gentile, great or small (Rom 10:12,13).

In his epistle to the Colossians, Paul declared his goal was to preach, warn, and teach, so that listeners might become complete in Christ. This means that those he taught could reproduce themselves in others.

It is important for preachers and Christians to warn unbelievers of the imminent judgment coming upon unrepentant sinners when we preach to them (Ezek. 3:18; Matt. 3:36).

d.   **To invite everyone to Christ**
There is an open invitation for sinners to repent and receive Jesus Christ as their Lord and Saviour. God has no interest in the death or destruction of a sinner.

In His invitation to everyone for abundant life God, speaking through Isaiah, said:

Ho! Everyone who thirsts, come to the waters, and you who have no money, come buy and eat. Yes, come, buy wine and milk without money and without price.
(Isaiah 55:1)

The Meaning of Salvation

Salvation is an all-inclusive word- a biblical and theological term-which embraces all the redemptive blessings which we receive in Christ. These include: regeneration, justification, adoption and sanctification. Salvation is a comprehensive term which covers all the redemptive blessings we receive through our relationship with Jesus Christ.

The word "salvation" is from the Greek noun "Soteria"- from the verb "sozo", to save, to rescue, to deliver, to heal or to make whole – which denotes deliverance, salvation, healthy preservation. Christ is the Divine "Soter", the Deliverer or Defender, Saviour, Preserver (see: Luke 2:11; John 4:42; Acts 5:31; 13:23; Tit. 1:4: 3:6 etc.).

From this Greek word "Soteria", "Soteriology", the theological term for the doctrine of Salvation has been derived. In the Bible, the word "salvation" is not necessarily used in a technical theological term but simply denotes "deliverance" from evil material or spiritual, sin, sickness, enemy, battle, danger. Thus, "deliver us from evil" is synonymous with "save us from evil". In a theological sense, however, Salvation denotes "(1) the whole process by which man is delivered from all that interferes with the enjoyment of God's highest blessings (2) the actual enjoyment of those blessings". [12]

According to W. E. Vine:

Salvation is used in the New Testament (a) of material and temporal deliverance from danger and apprehension, (1) national, Luke 1:69, 71; Acts 7:25... (2) Personal, as from the sea, Acts 27:34; prison, Phil. 1:19; the flood, Heb 11:7; (b) of spiritual and eternal deliverance granted immediately by God to those who accept His conditions of repentance and faith in the Lord Jesus, in whom alone it is to be obtained, Acts 4:12, and upon confession of Him as Lord, Rom. 10:10... (c) of the present experience of God's power to deliver from the bondage of sin, e.g. Phil. 2:12... 1 Pet. 1:9; this present experience on the part of believers is virtually equivalent to sanctification... (d) of the future deliverance of believers at the Parousia of Christ for His saints, a salvation which is the object of their confident and hope, eg., Rom. 13:11; 1 Thess 5:8, and ver. 9, where salvation is assured to them as being deliverance from the wrath of God destined to be executed upon the ungodly at the end of this age (see: 1 Thess 1:10). [13]

The equivalent Hebrew word, "Yeshuah", conveys a similar meaning as deliverance from evil or danger. This deliverance may be from defeat in battle (Exd.14:13; 15:2; 2 Chron 20:17), trouble (Psalm 34:6), enemies (2 Sam. 3:10, Psalm 18:3), violence

---

12. Steven Barabas, "Salvation", an article in Zondervern Pictorial Bible Dictionary, Miichigan: Zondervern Publishing House, 1967, P. 743.
13. W. E. Vine, Vine's Expository Dictionary of New Testament Words, Massachusetts: Hendrickson Publications, (no date), P. 998.

(2 Sam. 22:3), reproach (Psalm 57:3), exile (Psalm 106:47), death (Psalm 6:4) and sin, (Ezek 36:29). The deliverance of the children of Israel from Egypt is an outstanding example of divine salvation in the early history of Israel.

Since Jehovah is the provider of this deliverance, He is often spoken of as Saviour (Isa. 43:3,11; 45:15; 49:26; Jer. 14:8). This title is usually applied to Jesus in the New Testament (Luke 2:11; John 4:42; Acts 5:31 etc).

In the teaching of Jesus, salvation is often used to denote "deliverance" from evil or trouble – like sickness (Matt. 9:22; Mark 5:34; Luke 8:48). But it is usually used to denote deliverance from sin, including its causes and consequences, which is received by faith in His redemptive sacrifice.

Salvation from sin is the primary purpose and blessing of the atonement; healing- both divine healing and divine health-and other physical or material blessings of the atonement may be viewed as secondary.

But He was wounded for our transgressions, He was bruised for our iniquities; the Chastisement for our peace was upon Him. And by His stripes we are healed. (Isaiah 53:5; See also: Matt. 8:17; 1 Pet. 2:24; cp. Psalm 103:1-5).

Salvation, through Christ, is the central theme of the entire Apostolic Age. It is represented primarily as deliverance from sin. This salvation is obtained only through Jesus Christ (Acts 4:12), upon confession of Him as Lord and Saviour (Rom. 10:10). The entire New Testament lays emphasis on the suffering and death of Jesus Christ as mediating salvation (Eph. 2:13-18).

Repentance and faith in Jesus Christ are conditions for this salvation and the gospel is the saving instrument (Rom. 1:16; Eph. 1:13).

In line with the teaching of Jesus Christ, the apostles represent salvation as a present experience, though it is eschatological as well; that is, we can be saved now, as well as in future. But the present is necessary for future or eternal deliverance. One must be saved now, and remain saved in this present life, in order to enjoy the full blessedness of eternal life. The blessings of salvation we experience now are only a foretaste of what we will experience in the coming age, when Christ comes to establish His Kingdom.

Saving Grace

Salvation is given by God to be received by men. On the human side, salvation is made possible through faith; this is known as "saving faith" – the faith by which salvation is received. The sinner is to do the "believing" in order to receive God's saving grace.

Paul said sinners are saved by grace, received through faith (Eph. 2:8, 9) and are created to do good works (Eph. 2:10).

For by grace you have been saved through faith, and that not of yourselves; it is the gift of God, not of works, lest anyone should boast.
(Ephesians 2:8, 9)

Turning His ministry over to His disciples, Jesus commanded them "to preach the gospel to every creature; he who believes and is baptized will be saved; but he who does not believe will be condemned" (Mark 16:16).

Similarly Paul and Silas told the Philippian Jailor; "Believe on the Lord Jesus Christ, and you will be saved; you and your household" (Acts. 16:31).

This is not just a mental assent to some doctrinal statements, but a genuine repentance and whole hearted commitment to Christ as Lord and Saviour.

Paul communicates what to do to be saved for the sinner to be victorious in Romans 10:

But what does it say? The word is near you, in your mouth and in your heart (that is, the word of faith which we preach) that if you confess with your mouth the Lord Jesus and believe in your heart that God has raised Him from the dead, you will be saved. For with the heart one believes unto righteousness, and with the mouth confession is made unto salvation.
(Romans 10:8-10)

On the part of God, the ultimate course of salvation is the grace or mercy of God. It is unmerited, underserved, and totally devoid of human effort; for salvation is by grace alone.

Scriptural basis and evidences

Salvation by grace is stressed positively and profoundly in the New Testament.

Paul took time to reflect on our past failures and God's present redemption. He said that God not only raised Jesus up and sat Him in heavenly places above all authority (Eph. 2:20), but He did the same for us (Eph. 2:4-6).

Even when we were dead in trespasses, he made us alive together with Christ (by grace you have been saved).
                              (Ephesians 2:5)

In Romans 3:24, Paul described God's righteousness through faith when he wrote: "being justified freely by His grace through the redemption that is in Christ Jesus".

In Romans 11:6, Paul reminds us that we are saved by grace, not by works, merit or self-worth because if it is by works, it is no longer grace.

And if by grace, then it is no longer of works, otherwise grace is no longer grace. But if it is of works, it is no longer grace, otherwise work is no longer work.

Titus 2:11 makes us realize that we are trained by saving grace to live righteously.

For the grace of God that brings salvation has appeared to all men, teaching us that, denying ungodliness and worldly lusts, we should live soberly, righteously, and godly in the present age.

Paul went further in Titus 3:6-7 to remind us that God the Father is the author of our salvation and saves us by Jesus Christ. He highlighted the purpose of saving us which is to justify us through faith at our regeneration and make us righteous by daily renewing of the Holy Ghost by His grace as opposed to works (Titus 3:5), that we should be made heirs **"according to hope of eternal life"**.

The doctrine of saving grace is beautifully presented in the well-known hymn, "Amazing Grace", by John Newton (1725-1805), published in 1779. Newton was a captain of a slave ship for many years, until he was converted. He devoted his life to Christ and His service and wrote many Christian hymns, including "Amazing Grace".

Amazing grace,
How sweet the sound,
That saved a wretch like me!
I once was lost
But now I 'm found,
Was blind but now I see.

It was grace that taught
My heart to fear,
And grace my fears relieved;
How precious did that grace appear
The hour I first believed.

Through many dangers,
Toils and snare,
I have already come.
T'is grace that brought me safe thus far,
And grace will lead me home.

The following are some scriptural basis and distinguishing marks of saving grace.

a.   **It is available to all**

Saving grace is available to all men-all sinners can receive God's grace for salvation. Since the atonement is universal – that is, Christ died for all men (Heb 2:9), God has made provision for all men to be saved in the atonement (John 3:15-17). He has given "opportunity to all men everywhere to repent" (Acts 17:30), because He would like all men to be saved.

Who desires all men to be saved and come to the knowledge of the truth.
(1 Timothy 2:4)

Moreover, His grace is available for all men to be saved; anyone who desires to be saved can be saved from sin.

For the grace of God that brings salvation has appeared to all men, teaching us that, denying ungodliness and worldly lusts, we should live soberly, righteously and godly in the present age.
(Titus 2:11)

b.   **It is abundantly available**
There is no limit to saving grace, where sin and sinners are concerned, there is abundant grace for every sin. No sin is too great that cannot be forgiven, as human sins abound more grace abounds to save from sin.

Moreover the law entered that offence might abound. But where sin abounded, grace abounded much more, so that as sin reigned in death, even so grace might reign through righteousness to eternal life through Jesus Christ our Lord. (Romans 5:20-21)

However, the availability of God's grace must not be taken for granted; it must not be used as an excuse for conscious sinning or careless living.

What shall we say then? Shall we continue in sin that grace may abound? Certainly not. How shall we who died to sin live any longer in it?
(Romans 6:1-2)

c.   **It is not earned by works of righteousness**
Saving grace is entirely unmerited, it is not earned by our works of righteousness. While good work should be encouraged – as a demonstration of faith in action (Jam 2:14-20), works alone are insufficient to earn saving grace. All our works-apart from the grace of God - to earn salvation, are like "filthy rags" (Isa. 64:6).

We are saved by grace alone not by our works. Paul argued in Roman 11:6 that there are two possible sources of salvation- men's works and God's grace - the two are essentially distant and opposite.

He explained that salvation cannot be a mixture of both but must be wholly either of one or the other. In Ephesians 2:8-9, Paul makes it clear that salvation is by God's grace, not of works so that no man should glory.

Paul concluded:
Not by works of righteousness which we have done, but according to His mercy He saved us, through the washing of regeneration and renewing of the Holy Spirit.
(Titus 3:5)

d.   **It is sufficient in all situations**
The grace of God is sufficient – it is enough to save everyone, for every situation, irrespective of culture or race or occasion or status.

My grace is sufficient for you, for my strength is made perfect in weakness.
(2 Corinthians 12:9)

The Bible speaks of the richness or "riches" of divine grace; God is rich in mercy (Eph. 2:4), and His grace is invaluable (Eph. 1:7, 18). Therefore, His grace is greater than our sins; it is rich enough to save us and keep us saved even "to the uttermost" (Heb. 7:25).

e.   **It is freely given**
Saving grace is given freely, it is not earned or paid for; it is free of charge.

Paul wrote to Christians in Rome:

Being justified freely by grace through the Redemption that is in Christ Jesus.
(Rom. 3:24; KJV).

The Greek adverb "dorean" is used here for "freely". It denotes "gratuitously", that is, given freely, not earned or paid for. It stresses the grace of the Giver. It demonstrates His act of graciousness in the scheme of redemption towards fallen humanity and salvation towards sinful humanity.

All the blessings we enjoy in the redemptive plan of God are given freely, without price.

The call of Gentiles to faith is the result of God's grace to the Jews first before He extended the universal invitation to whosoever will receive the free salvation without money (Isa. 55:1). Jesus warned the disciples as He sent them out to preach the gospel freely, not to commercialize all the works of grace. As they received freely they should carry out their assignment without cost to the people (Matt. 10:8).

Jesus promised to restore freely what we lost in the Garden of Eden in His vision to John

...It is done! I am the Alpha and Omega the Beginning and the End, I will give of the fountain of the water of life freely to Him who thirsts.
(Rev. 21:6; 22:17)

Saving grace is free, it is "free gift" from God to sinners. It is given as an act of God's loving kindness and mercy to His creatures. It is one of the "free gifts" given to us by God (Rom 5:15, 15, 16, 18).

Paul argues theologically for free grace; that since God – in His justice-did not spare His Son, but gave Him up for us all, He can give us all things "freely"- including saving grace.

He who did not spare His own Son, but deliver Him up for us all, how shall He not with Him also freely give us all things.
(Romans 8:32)

f.   **It is given without discrimination**
Saving grace places all men on the same level in the sight of God. There is no discrimination where grace

for salvation is concerned. Since we all share "common faith" (Tit. 1:4) and "common salvation" (Jude 3), we all share the same "common grace", to receive this "common salvation". Since "all have sinned" (Rom. 3:23) and all men have been "concluded under sin" (Gal. 3:22), all men need the same divine mercy (Rom 11:32), without discrimination. God is not partial, He is "no respecter of persons" (Acts 10:34-35; see also: Acts 10:12; Eph. 6:9). He treats everyone equally in dispensing Divine justice. In Him all distinctions are lost. There is no distinction between rich and poor, male or female, Greek or Gentile. All are sinners, all deserve death (Rom 6:23) and all are given same grace for "common salvation".

To make plain his teaching on salvation, Paul used stories to drive home the truth, he used an illustration of Abraham:

And the scripture, foreseeing that God would justify the Gentiles by faith, preached the gospel to Abraham beforehand, saying "in you all the nations will be blessed": There is neither Jew nor Greek, there is neither slave nor free, there is neither male nor female you are all one in Christ.

(Galatians 3:8, 28)

Paul also wrote:

Where there is neither Greek nor Jew, circumcised nor uncircumcised, barbarian, Scythian, slave nor free, but Christ is all and in all.

(Colossians 3:11)

Thus, there is unity of divine life shared by all believers, which counter balances all differences. Christianity imparts to the most uncivilized the only spring of sound, social and moral culture.

CHAPTER 5

SUFFICIENT AND STRENGTHENING GRACE

In Paul's second epistle to the Corinthians, he robustly defended his apostleship in chapters 10-12. He made reference to his apostolic proofs, personal sufferings and sacrifices "for the sake of Christ" and his personal spiritual experiences and supernatural encounters – in heavenly realms.

The twelfth chapter is devoted to his vision and thorn in the flesh.

It is doubtless not profitable for me to boast. I will come to visions and revelations of the Lord: I know a man in Christ who fourteen years ago- whether in the body I do not know or whether out of the body I do not know, God knows-such a one was caught up to the third heaven.
(2 Corinthians 12:1-2)

Paul received "abundance of revelation" in his vision, and to keep him from becoming proud, he was given a thorn in the flesh. A messenger of Satan was sent to torment him, with a thorn in the flesh, so that according to him, "lest I be exalted above measure".

And lest I should be exalted above measure by the abundance of the revelations, a thorn in the flesh was given to me, a messenger of Satan to buffet me, lest I be exalted above measure.
(2 Corinthians 12:7)

We have no record in the Scripture of what this "thorn in the flesh" was; we can only speculate. Some scholars believe it was blindness, others feel it was malaria or constant beating by opponents of the gospel. Whatever it was, it was obviously an affliction which touched his body-an affliction permitted by God, to make him uncomfortable. It was an encumbrance to his ministry.

Job had a similar experience as Paul's, Satan was permitted to afflict him, at the height of his glory and prosperity. Job was a man of strong character, industrious, discerning, devoted to God and family, and well-thought-of by people. The Bible describes Job as "blameless and upright, a man who shuns evil". He had the reputation for integrity, a leadership model in his community. A twist came in the life of Job when Satan attacked his character:

Then God asked Satan: "Have you considered My servant Job, that there is none like him on the earth, blameless and upright man, one who fears God and shuns evil?" Satan said: "Does Job fear God for nothing? Have You not made a hedge around him, around his household, and around all that he has on every side? You have blessed the works of his hand, and his possessions have increased in the land. But now, stretch out your hand and touch all that he has, and he will surely curse You to Your face!"

(Job 1:8-10).

In order to prove the uprightness and integrity of Job, God permitted Satan to destroy "all that he had, only do not lay a hand on his person". Job lost everything he had, including his ten children (Job 1:13-19). After suffering all these calamities, Job did not deny God, "he fell to the ground and worshipped".

Job made God proud having justified the confidence God reposed in him; Again God told Satan: "Have you considered My servant Job, that there is none like him on the earth, a blameless and upright man, one who fears God and shuns evil…" (Job 2:3).

Satan was not satisfied, he told God that a man can use material things to redeem his life. He sought permission from God to afflict Job with pains that he will surely deny God. He was given the permission and "Satan struck Job with painful boils from the sole of his foot to the crown of his head" (Job 2:4-7). "In all this, Job did not sin with his lips".

Concerning Paul, this was not the first time that Satan hindered Paul.

For a great and effective door has opened to me, and there are many adversaries.
(1 Corinthians 16:9)

Writing to the Thessalonian church, Paul complained:

"We wanted to come to you-even I Paul, time and again- but Satan hindered".
(1 Thessalonians 2:18).

In his epistle to Timothy, Paul told Timothy about the harm done to him by Alexander (2 Timo 4: 14-17).

But this "thorn in the flesh" caused him great pain and discomfort; he prayed for its removal, to no avail.

This was a difficult time for Paul- a time of great challenges and trial of faith. It is easy to trust God in good times, but very challenging to believe God in rough times, especially when we have totally obeyed Him. This is where the grace of God is needed most. Faith and courage may fail, but grace will strengthen us. Human strength and resources are limited and helpless when challenges are humanly unbearable; for "by strength shall no man prevail" (1 Sam 2:9).

God's grace is able to see us through all challenges. It is sufficient for all human needs.

And God is able to make grace abound toward you, that you, always having all sufficiency in all things, may have abundance for every good work.
(2 Corinthians 9:8)

Thrice Paul prayed for the thorn to be removed, but God did not remove it. Instead, he was assured of greater blessings; God gave him "greater grace" to endure his afflictions, a stronger character, humility and the ability to encourage others, even in his afflictions. Thus, he could say:

Therefore I endure all things for the sake of the elect that they also may obtain the salvation which is in Christ Jesus with eternal glory.
(2 Timothy 2:10)

Again, he said:

As unknown, and yet well known; as dying and behold we live; as chastened, and yet not killed; as sorrowful, yet always rejoicing; as poor, and yet making rich; as having nothing, and yet possessing all things.
(2 Corinthians 6:9-10)

The Lord gave Paul this answer:

My grace is sufficient for thee and my strength is made perfect in weakness.
(2 Corinthians 12:9a)

Although God did not remove Paul's "thorn", He did not ignore His servant's affliction; He provided special grace to help him endure his trouble. He promised to demonstrate His power through the sufficiency of His grace and it's strengthening power. His grace releases strength to perfect our imperfections (Psalm 138:8) and make possible our impossibilities.

Paul accepted God's will, and in total submission, he said:

...Therefore most gladly I will rather boast in my infirmities, that the power of Christ may rest upon me. Therefore I take pleasure in my infirmities, in reproaches, in needs, in persecutions, in distress, for Christ's sake. For when I am weak, then I am strong.
(2 Corinthians 12: 9b-10).

From these two scriptural texts, two effects of divine grace are clearly revealed:

1. Sufficiency of Grace: "My grace is sufficient for thee..." (vs 9a)

2. Strengthening Grace: "My strength is made perfect in weakness... when I am weak then I am strong" (vs 9b,10).

Grace for Sufficiency

Divine grace is sufficient enough to meet all our human needs. It is strong enough to support us in every great challenge we face. God is "able to make all grace abound towards" us, so that we can always have "all sufficiency in all things".

And God is able... to make grace abound toward you, that you, always having all sufficiency in all things may have abundance for every good work.
(2 Corinthians 9:8)

The word sufficiency means: **Being sufficient, ability, efficiency, adequate resources, competence, a sufficient amount...** [14]

Divine grace provides us with divine resources that are far more than what our natural resources can cope with. It is to us, as "shock absorber" is to a car. Thus, we can go through anything – battles, afflictions, crisis, challenges – all because of His enabling of grace.

Thus, we can say, like Paul:

I can do all things through Christ who strengthens me.
(Philippians 4:13)

Paul used the Greek verb "arkeo" for "sufficient" in 2 Cor. 12:9; which denotes to be strong enough, to be enough for a thing, to suffice, to be possessed of sufficient strength. It is also translated "sufficeth" (John 14:8), "sufficient" (John 6:7; 2 Cor. 12:9),

---
14. Concise English Dictionary London: Oxford University press, 1961, P. 1291.

"Enough" (Matt. 25:9) and "content" (Luke 3:14; 1 Timo. 6:8).

Paul used the word- both in the noun and adjective forms- in his second letter to the Corinthians. "And who is sufficient for these things?" (2 Cor. 2:16). That is, "who is adequate for this task as this?".

Again, he said:

Not that we are sufficient of ourselves to think anything as of ourselves; but our sufficiency is of God.
(2 Cor. 3:5 KJV).

That is, without the grace of God, we become "insufficient" or "deficient" we do not have enough resources by ourselves, but our sufficiency is of God. God is the source of our sufficiency, ability and resources. And His grace makes us sufficient, making our natural insufficiencies to become supernaturally sufficient. Paul used the Greek adjective "Hikanos" for "sufficient" in 2 Cor. 2:16 and 2 Cor. 3:5, which means enough, fit, sufficient, able or worthy or competent. He also used the noun form, "Hikanotes", for "sufficiency" in 2 Cor. 3:5, which denotes competence, ability, sufficient amount. Thus, "we can do all things through" the sufficient grace of God (Phil 4:13).

Divine grace is sufficiently powerful to lift us up when we are down, to keep us going, when the going gets tough, to surmount obstacles and face challenges with courage.

Without God's sufficient grace, we would become "deficient", break down or bow out. But grace keeps us in the race, strong in battle, competent for ministry and confident in challenges.

In spite of all his challenges and seemingly uncomfortable conditions caused by his "thorns", Paul was able to say:

Who shall separate us from the love of Christ? shall tribulation, or distress, or persecution, or famine, or nakedness, or peril, or sword? As it is written: "For Your sake we are killed all day long. We are accounted as sheep for the slaughter". Yet in all these things we are more than conquerors through Him who loved us.
(Romans 8:35-37)

Strengthening Grace

The second effect of grace in 2 Cor. 12:9-10 is "strengthening grace"; "my strength is made perfect in weakness … when I am weak, then am I strong". This grace is linked with the "enough grace" in vs 9a. The grace of God makes us "strong" inside, even when we are weak outside. Satan may afflict our bodies with "thorns", yet, because of God's grace, we can be divinely renewed inwardly.

This was Stephen's experience; when his persecutors stoned him, he was enabled by God's grace, to pray for them. The grace strengthened him inwardly, though the physical body was dying.

And they cast him out of the city and stoned him. And the witnesses laid down their clothes at the feet of a young man named Saul. And they stoned Stephen as he was calling on God and saying; "Lord Jesus receive my spirit".

Then he knelt down and cried out with a loud voice, "Lord do not charge them with this sin". And when he had said this, he fell asleep.
(Acts 7: 58-60)

As humans, we are not invisible or supernatural. We have infirmities, weaknesses, and imperfections. Even the strongest among us can be weak, tired, fail, fall or falter. But God can renew our strength, so that we can soar with wings like eagles.

He gives power to the weak and to those who have no might He increases strength. Even the youths shall faint and be weary, and the young men shall utterly fall. But those who wait on the Lord shall renew their strength; they shall mount up with wings like eagles, they shall run and not be weary, they shall walk and not faint.
(Isaiah 40:29-31)

Our natural strength is totally insufficient to sustain us in tough times. Those who trust in their strength will fail; "for by strength shall no man prevail" (1 Sam. 2:9).

God is the Source of our strength

David in an exuberant declaration of faith, acknowledged God as his strength. Strength here means power, influence, dominance, clout; God is the greatest pillar of support any man can have.

David wrote:
The Lord is my light an my salvation; whom shall I fear? The Lord is the strength of my life; of whom shall I be afraid.
(Psalm 27:1).

David also wrote:

God is my strength and power, and he makes my way perfect.
(2 Samuel 22:33)

The Psalmist in Psalm 46 referred to God as the refuge (a place of trust) of His people and conqueror of the nations, a present help, a help He has been found exceedingly (Psalm 46:1).

At the end of his letter to the Ephesians, Paul warned them about the tough times his people will face. They were up against Satan (Eph. 6:12), an enemy who will do everything to stop their progress. Instead of getting worried about the situation Paul admonished them not to approach this fight in their own strength, but remember only God can defeat the enemy.

Finally brethren, be strong in the Lord and in the power of His might.
(Ephesians 6:10).

Only the joy of the Lord can restore true strength to your life, especially when you remember your past sin, failures and aftermath of your disappointments and frustrations (Nehe. 8:10).

God is the Giver of strength

It is God who has given us power-might, ability, strength- to succeed.

And you shall remember the Lord your God, for it is he who gives you power to get wealth, that

He may establish His covenant which He swore to your fathers, as it is this day.
(Deuteronomy 8:18)

God has promised to give us strength

Strength is stamina, grit, backbone, fortitude, toughness, tenacity or will-power; God is the giver of strength to overcome every difficulty. He gives power to them that do faint and renews the strength of the weak. In Isa 40:31, God promised to renovate those who wait for him, they shall put forth fresh feathers as eagles so that they can soar high.

Speaking through Isaiah, God assured believers of His help in Isaiah 41:

Fear not, for I am with you, be not dismayed, for I am your God. I will strengthen you, yes, I will help you, I will uphold you with My righteous right hand.
(Isaiah 41:10)

But Daniel reminds us that only those who know their God (those who trust Him) will be strong and do exploits. (Daniel 11:32b)

Even in our weaknesses, there is Divine strength. So manifest are God's perfections, that by very weak instruments, He conclusively sets forth His praise.

This picture is vividly painted in Psalm 8:2, where infants are not only wonderful illustrations of God's power and skill, but also, in their physical constitution, instincts and early developed intelligence, and in their spontaneous admiration of

God's work in which they put to shame men who rail against God.

Out of mouth of babes and nursing infants You have ordained strength, that you may silence the enemies and the avenger.
(Psalm 8:2)

In Isaiah 40:29-31, God confirms that He is the source of every need we may have. We are all dependent on Him including the weak and the strong illustrated by 'young men' who are picked on account of their youthful vigour. This is why the scripture says; "by separating yourself from me you can do nothing".

Paul relished his weaknesses because he was convinced that the tougher his problems, the greater the grace (2 Cor. 12:10). Therefore, we should not rely on our physical strength or gifts, neither should we be discouraged by our weaknesses which are visible but we should rely more on the inner man, the Holy Spirit who is invisible and is being daily renewed in us.

Paul reminds us that the exploits of the heroes and heroines of faith were not achieved by their strength but "out of weaknesses they were made strong".

Who through faith subdued kingdoms, worked righteousness, obtained promises, stopped the mouths of lions, quenched the violence of fire, escaped the edge of the sword, out of weakness they were made strong, became valiant in battle, turned to flight the armies of the aliens.
(Hebrew 11:33-34)

The grace of God is the channel of divine strength. In the time of weakness or discouragement, we can "confess" that we are strong.

In the last chapter of his book, Joel pronounced judgment on nations and declared hope for God's people; if Judah will respond with obedience, God would use them to judge the nations.

Proclaim this among the nations: Prepare for war! Wake up the mighty men, let all the men of war draw near, let them come up... let the weak say, I am strong.
(Joel 3:9-10)

In spite of our weaknesses and shortcomings, if we respond to God in obedience, He will renew our strength and use us to do exploits and make accomplishments in all our endeavours (2 Cor. 12:10).

To be strong in the Lord (Eph. 6:10), is to be strong in the grace that is given by the Lord.

Paul encouraged Timothy to be strong in grace.

You therefore, my son, be strong in the grace that is in Christ Jesus.
(2 Timothy 2:1)

The grace of God can strengthen you when you are weak.

a.) David found strength in the Lord
In 1 Samuel 30: 1-6, life became distasteful to David when the houses he was living with his 600 followers was burnt down by the Amalekites and their children

and wives taken captives. Even his aggrieved subordinates wept and thought of stoning him, but this appeared as the end of the road for David as a leader. David refused to surrender to emotion but saw what befell them as a temporary set-back. He took the challenges to God and asked God to proffer solution to their predicament.

In verse 6, David "encouraged himself in the Lord". Thus he received divine strength.

b.) Paul was divinely strengthened by God when he faced challenges at the later part of his life.

But the Lord stood with me and strengthened me, so that the message might be preached through me, and that all the Gentiles might hear. Also I was delivered out of the mouth of the lion.
(2 Timothy 4:17)

c.) Paul testified concerning the source of his strength and the faithfulness of God.

I can do all things through Christ who strengthens me.
(Philippians 4:13).

d.) Elijah's strength was divinely renewed to continue in ministry
It was ironic that Elijah would flee from Jezebel after a great revival which reconciled the people to God. The courageous leader who single-handedly faced 450 prophets of Baal took to his heels and ran from a wicked woman who threatened his life. (1 Kings 19: 1-5)

Though Elijah was burnt-out, full of emotions, God did not forsake him but encouraged him and provided him with food to strengthen him:

Then he looked, and there by his head was a cake baked on coals, and a jar of water. So he ate and drank, and lay down again.
(1 Kings 19:6).

God can release His grace at this moment of your challenges. His grace is both sufficient and strengthening. In your present predicament, do not give up hope, repose your confidence in the Lord. Like David, encourage yourself in the Lord. You will surely receive fresh strength to forge ahead. This is your day of renewal for exploits.

CHAPTER 6

SERVING GRACE

While all Christians have "saving grace", not every Christian has "serving grace", though it is available for every Christian.

Serving grace is the supernaturally bestowed favour to serve God and His church beyond our natural abilities or resources, in a way that is pleasing or acceptable to Him.

It takes more than natural or intellectual powers to serve God – not in our own way or by worldly standards – but in God's own way; that is, in the way that pleases and honours Him. One thing is to serve God, another thing is to serve Him acceptably; it takes the grace of God to do this.

Paul wrote to the Hebrew Christians and, indeed, to the modern church:

Wherefore we receiving a Kingdom which cannot be shaken, let us have grace, by which we may serve God acceptably with reverence and godly fear.

(Hebrews 12:28)

The above scripture clearly reveals two basic facts about serving grace:

1. The grace for serving: "Let us have grace, whereby we may serve God".

2. The purpose of serving grace:
(a) To serve God acceptably
(b) To serve God reverently

(c) To serve God with Godly fear.

The Grace for Service

To serve means to do service or to do the work of God. Every religious activity or assignment or duty we do towards God and His church is "service". The Greek word used here is not the usual Greek word for "to serve" (that is, diakoneo, which means to serve, to minister); the Greek word Latreuo is the word used for "serve" in Heb, 12:28. It means "to offer service". Thus, "that we may serve", denotes "that we may offer service to God". The word is translated "serve" (Matt. 4:10), "that we might serve him without fear" (Luke 1:74; see also: Acts 7:7; 27:23; Rom. 1:9; 2 Tim 1:3; Heb. 8:5; 9:14; 12:28; 13:10 etc), service (Heb. 9:9), serving (Acts 26:7).

It is also translated "worship" (Act 7:2; 24:14; Phil 3:3), worshippers (Heb. 10:2). We are told that Anna, a prophetess, an 84 years old widow:

Departed not from the temple but served God with fastings and prayers night and day.
(Luke 2:37)

The Greek word is used primarily of service rendered towards God. Thus, it is more related with worship, than public ministration. However, I would use the word "service" in a general sense to include our personal service towards God and the services we render, on His behalf, towards the church. In this sense, every work we do on God's behalf or "in the Lord's name" is a "service". All these service require divine grace to please God or render it acceptably.

Grace is needed for Service
Our service towards God is not secular, but spiritual; therefore, we need His grace to do His work supernaturally, in a way that will please Him.

Paul tells us: "**that those who are in the flesh cannot please God**" (Rom 8:8). That is, those who attempt to serve God with their natural abilities cannot please God. He also says that "**without faith it is impossible to please God**" (Heb 11:6). We must "**worship God in the spirit**", so that we may rejoice in Christ (Phil. 3:3). This is the function of Divine grace in service; Grace provides all we need to serve God acceptably – which include: faith, power, wisdom, and supernatural resources.

The children of Israel served the Lord, but not with a joyful spirit. Their service did not honour God, because they lacked the grace for such service. Therefore, the Lord placed a curse on them.

Because you did not serve the Lord your God with joy and gladness of heart, for the abundance of everything, therefore, you shall serve your enemies, whom the Lord will send against you, in hunger, in thirst, in nakedness and in need of everything; and He will put a yoke of iron on your neck until He has destroyed you.
(Deuteronomy 28:47, 48)
In his valedictory message, Joshua spoke frankly to the children of Israel. He said:

You cannot serve the LORD; for He is a holy God; He is a jealous God; He will not forgive your transgressions nor your sins.
(Joshua 24:19).

In other words, Joshua was simply saying, "you cannot serve God by His standard because you do not possess the grace to live up to His expectations". Although they insisted that they could and would serve the Lord (Josh. 24:21-24), they failed God many times and incurred His wrath. Paul made reference to the failings and failure of the children of Israel; he said:

But with most of them God was not well pleased, for their bodies were scattered in the wilderness.
                              (1 Corinthians 10:5)

Serving without Grace

It is not possible for Christians to serve God without His grace, depending on their own resources. It is difficult to please God without His favour (see Heb. 11:6; 12:28). Those who serve without grace, will be disgraced and frustrated. No Christian can succeed in service by his own strength (I Sam. 2:9); our services are unacceptable except when it is performed through the grace given to us.

Those who serve God without His grace may appear to be successful, but, to God, they are not recognized. Jesus spoke about this in Mathew Chapter 7:

Not everyone who says to Me, 'Lord, Lord,' shall enter the Kingdom of heaven, but he who does the will of My father in heaven. Many will say to Me in that day, 'Lord, Lord, have we not prophesied in Your name, cast out demons in Your name, and done many wonders in Your

name? 'And then I will declare to them,' I never knew you, depart from Me you who practice lawlessness.

(Mathew 7:21-23)

Characteristics of graceless service

According to Jesus, "by their fruits we shall know them" (Matt. 7:20). The following are some of the fruits of graceless services:

a.) Divided loyalty
Divided means split, disunited, alienated, estranged, while loyalty means faithfulness, commitment, devotion, dutiful, unwavering. Divided loyalty is to set at variance to the true service of God. A person with a divided loyalty lacks commitment and shares his love between God and terrestrial things. A servant cannot serve two masters.

b.) Grudging Spirit
A person with grudging spirit is one who is reluctant, unwilling or unenthusiastic in rending service to God. He is half-hearted in anything he does for God. Such service is unacceptable to God.

c.) Eye Service
Eye service is the service a person renders with a view to pleasing men and create false impression, as a pretender, to be an effective worker. The Bible enjoins servants to do their work as if they were doing it for God and not as if expecting reward or praise from men, their masters (Colossians 3:22).

d.) Inconsistency
To be inconsistent is to be unpredictable, changeable and unsteady. No one can rely or trust an

inconsistent person, he changes like a chameleon. He is unpredictable, his next move or action is dictated by his mood and not by the inspiration of the Holy Spirit.

e.) Suffering in Silence
This situation arises when a person is going through hardship, pains or inconveniences and refuses to share his ordeal with anybody nor seek possible solution but pretends as if everything is alright. A person suffering in silence will have his psyche and morale shattered while his productivity will be at the lowest ebb. Consequently, he will not be able to serve God gracefully.

f.) Lack of Joy
A joyless person is unhappy, melancholic and depressed. No graceful service can come from such a mood. Even when he puts up courage and pretends to serve God, such service instead of being rewarded with blessing it will attract a curse (Deut 28:47, 48).

g.) Serving with Flesh
God cannot be served with the flesh because "**God is spirit and those who worship Him must worship Him in spirit and truth**" (John 4:24). Any service rendered in the flesh is not only unproductive, and 'unrewardable' but unacceptable to God because no man in the flesh can please God.

h.) Spiritual Pride
"Pride goes before destruction and a haughty spirit before a fall" (Proverbs 16:18). God is the source of all our earthly possessions, gifts, and all other heavenly endowments. We should use them and do everything to the glory of God (1 Cor. 10:31). We

should not commercialize His gifts but with humility we should serve Him and fellow mankind because He will never share His glory with any man. (Isa. 48:11).

i.) Unfaithful Spirit
Unfaithful spirit is a rebellious spirit which is not loyal to God. A man who serves God with unfaithful spirit will always render service with ulterior motive and such work will be counter-productive because it is geared towards personal motive.

j.) Half – heartedness
This is service rendered without commitment, obedience and loyalty. Service rendered to avoid criticism or rebuke from men is a half-hearted service. It is rendered without a goal or objective to please God. Any service rendered with an unwilling heart comes from half-heartedness.

k.) Over ambition
This is an inordinate aspiration in pursuit of a goal or position for self-aggrandizement. It is over ambition when a person wants to reach a particular position or serve at a particular level just for the purpose of drawing attention to himself, to boost his ego as opposed to rendering service to enrich the kingdom of God. Such service is not acceptable to God.

l.) Selfishness
To be selfish is to be self-willed and self-centred. A selfish person only works to please himself, he wants everything for himself. He wants to be adored, recognized, celebrated and given credit for everything. Even on the ground of morality, selfishness in men is regarded as the worst of all ill-manners. In the spiritual realm, a selfish person is

in competition with God, therefore his service can never be acceptable to Him.

m.) Over Confidence
An over confident person believes in his ability, competence, and capability to do all things. He does not need any body, including God, for assistance or input. Peter boasted, that he would never deny Jesus; "**Lord, I am ready to go with You, both to prison and to death**" (Luke 22:33). Eventually, he denied Jesus thrice before the next morning. The earlier prayer of Jesus saved the situation for Peter, he would have gone the way of Judas Iscariot (Luke 22: 31-37). Therefore, let repose our confidence in God who can deliver us from every unpleasant situation rather than relying on our abilities and arms of flesh.

n.) Disobedience
Disobedience is defiance or revolt against God's word or commandments. Disobedience means knowing what is right but doing contrary to it- recalcitrance. All the blessings of God are conditional upon our obedience to His injunctions (Deut. 28:1-14). Disobedience is rebellion against God and what he stands for. God views disobedience seriously, He often visits it with punishment. The scripture says; "For rebellion is as the sin of witchcraft, and stubbornness is as iniquity and idolatry, because you have rejected the word of the Lord, He also has rejected you from being king" (1 Sam. 15:23). Thus, God rejected Saul as the first king of Israel for the sin of disobedience. For our service to be acceptable to God, we must continuously live in obedience to His word.

o.) Lack of submission to spiritual authority
Christians are enjoined by the scripture to submit to authority both in the church and outside the church because **"there is no authority except from God, and the authorities that exist are appointed by God. Therefore whosoever resists the authority resists the ordinance of God, and those who resist will bring judgment on themselves"** (Rom. 13:1-2). There are three levels of submission (1) authority at home (Eph. 6:1; 5:22); (ii) civil authority (Rom. 13:1-7); (iii) authority in the church (Eph. 1:22).

Jesus puts it succinctly: "If a person cannot fear a man he sees, how can be fear God he does not see?" The service of a person who fails to submit to spiritual authority is unacceptable to the Lord.

p.) Presumptuous spirit
A presumptuous spirit is the one that is arrogant, insolent and conceited. He cannot bow or submit to the will of God. A worker who has presumptuous spirit is likely to be forward, rash and bigheaded. He will look down on everybody including those who are above him. God will not have anything to do with a man with presumptuous spirit.

q.) Lack of consecration
Consecration simply means to set something or someone apart for the peculiar service of the Lord. Therefore a person is said to lack consecration, when he is not committed, carnal or engaged in the service of God for personal reasons. Such worker is not chosen by God rather he has chosen himself, hence his work will be unproductive (John 15:16).

r.) Self pleasing / men pleasing

A person is said to be self-pleasing when his principal motive of working in the church is to please himself and not to please God. It may be because of material gain, ego-boosting or the personal pleasure he derives from such service.

On the other hand, a person is said to be men pleasing when his motive is to please men- who may be his admirers, or to win admiration, favour, or human praises from some people. The only acceptable service to God is the one rendered selflessly to enrich His kingdom and glorify His name.

s.) Hireling attitude

Hireling as used in the Bible means a labourer who receives pay (Job 7: 1-2; Isa. 16:14). In John 10:12-13, Jesus compared the owner of the sheep (shepherd) with the hireling. The hireling tends the sheep for money, but the true Shepherd does it out of love. The true owner of the flock leads them to and from pasturage and is ready to lay down his life for the sheep.

The message of our Lord Jesus here, is to demonstrate total commitment and sacrifice of a true owner (shepherd) to the sheep as compared to the hirelings who are merely working for a pay.

Doing the work of God requires total commitment, loyalty, and devotion. Our commitment should not be based on personal, dishonest gain or what will accrue to us in terms of money, ego-boosting or human praise (Pet. 5:1-4). Reward for acceptable service comes directly from the chief shepherd,

Jesus Christ; "For promotion cometh neither from the east, nor from the west, nor from the south. But God is the judge" (Psalm 75:6-7).

Example of Graceless Servants

a. Cain
Cain was the first man born naturally by Adam and Eve. Cain was the earth's first murderer who became jealous of the happiness of his brother, Abel, and his favour with God when He accepted his sacrifice and that of Cain was rejected. He yielded to his jealous feelings and slew Abel. Cain had himself to blame for using the product of his labour instead of animal for sacrifice (Gen. 4:3). Some Christians today trade blames for their failures and frustrations instead of engaging in self-examination and get reconciled to God (2 Cor. 13:5).

The wrath of God was upon Cain and God set a mark on him and he became a vagabond. Graceless servants will not only be punished but they will lose their reward.

b. Amaziah
Amaziah, son of Jehoash, king of Judah came to the throne after the assassination of his father. He made tremendous projects in his expeditions as God gave him victory over other nations. But he soon turned away from God and engaged in gross apostasy "**on return from the slaughter of the Edomites, that he brought the gods of the children of Seir, and set them up to be his gods, and bowed down himself before them and burned incense unto them**" (2 Chron. 25:14). Amaziah did what was pleasing to God, "but not with a perfect heart" (2 Chron. 25:2).

Just like Amaziah, some Christians who started well (2 Chrn. 25:2) have backslidden having been blessed or lifted up by God. The only solution is for such servants to reconcile to God through repentance (Prov. 28:13).

c. Lucifer
Lucifer, the most beautiful and the head of the angels in heaven, became proud and thought within himself to rebel and raise his kingdom above that of God. For his conspiracy with a third of the angels in heaven they were sent out of heaven and they fell unto the earth (Isa. 14: 12-14). Truly, pride goes before destruction..." (Prov. 16:18). Lucifer, now Satan, is an example of a servant who turned against His master and became an enemy who is out to destroy, kill and steal. He goes about with all ferocity, fury, power and grand deception as a prime enemy of mankind (1 Pet. 5:8). Christians have to look up to the Lord Jesus, the Author and Finisher of our faith, for succour and victory over Satan. (Heb. 12:2; 1 John 5:4-5).

d. Uzzah
Uzzah was a son of Abinadab who died for touching the Ark (2 Sam. 6: 3-8). The Ark should ordinarily be carried by Levites on stick. Levites were forbidden to touch the ark on threat of death (Num. 4: 15-20). The over zealousness of Uzzah was not an excuse. Doing a right thing in a wrong way is unacceptable to God. We should learn to do the right thing, the right way and at the right time, for our service to be acceptable.

e. King Saul
King Saul was the first king in Israel, even though he came from the smallest tribe, Benjamin, and the least in his family, God chose him. God raised him from grass to glory. Saul started well because he was anointed and filled with the Spirit but soon missed great opportunities and deliberately abused them. His sun rose in splendour, but set in a tragic night, he became disobedient (1 Sam. 15:10-23), self-willed and impatient, which restricted his influence (1 Sam. 13:12, 13) and was guilty of rash vows (1 Sam. 15:11-23). Jealousy prompted him to hunt and harm David (1 Sam. 18:8; 19:1). He patronized the superstition he had forbidden (1 Sam. 28:7). He was wounded in battle and ended up by committing suicide (1 Sam. 31:4). It is unfortunate that such sad story is repeated almost daily in this generation.

f. Demas
Demas was a companion of Paul during his first Roman imprisonment (Col. 4:14). The scripture recorded against him, "that he forsook Paul for this present world" (2 Timo. 4:10). Jesus says: "No one having put his hand to the plow and looking back, is fit for the kingdom of God" (Luke 9:62). Like Demas, many Church workers lack the grace to continue or endure to the end. It is only those Christians who persevere and endure to the end that will be saved.

g. Sons of Aaron
Nadab and Abihu, the sons of Aaron, "took either of them his censer, and put fire therein, and put incense thereon, and offered strange fire before the Lord, which He commanded them not" (Levit. 10:1). If we would worship and serve God acceptably, it must be in the way He has appointed (Col. 2:23).

We must worship God in humility, truth and spirit (John 4:24).

h. Judas Iscariot

Judas Iscariot was the disciple who betrayed Jesus Christ, having been with Him for three and half years, and then hanged himself. The Gospels present the betrayal of Christ, by Judas, as a horrible, diabolical crime. And it stands out as the darkest deed in human history. Christ became God-incarnate, Judas became the devil-incarnate; "one of you", said Jesus, "shall betray me" (Matt. 26:21). Apart from the scripture predicting his betrayal (Psa. 109:5-8; Zech 11:12-13), his lust for money reached a peak that he stole from the purse as the treasurer (John 12:6). He was compensated with money to betray Jesus with a kiss. As Christians we should be careful and watch out for lust of the eyes, lust of the flesh and pride of life (1 John 2:15-17). Jesus warned: **"Take heed and beware of covetousness, for one's life does not consist in the abundance of the things he possesses"** (Luke 12:15).

i. Sons of Eli

Hophini and Phinehas were the sons of Eli, the high priest and judge, who proved unworthy of sacred offices because he failed to discipline his sons (1 Sam. 1:3; 2:34; 4:4, 11, 17). The two sons of Eli were partners in evil practices and brought a twice-pronounced curse upon their heads (1 Sam. 2:34; 3:13). Both disgraced their priestly office by claiming and appropriating more than their due of the sacrifices (1 Sam. 2:13-17). They were both involved in immoral actions in the Tabernacle (1 Sam. 2:22). Both were slain at the battle of Aphek and this, coupled with the loss of the Ark, caused the death of Eli.

For every action there is a reaction, both brothers were disgraced and punished for their graceless services. This is a lesson for all Christian parents, especially ministers of God. They should take adequate care of the needs of their children including their education. They should not spare the rod when it is appropriate. Discipline should be maintained in the family without giving special preference to any child.

j. Prophet Balaam
Balaam, regarded as prophet, yet followed the unholy practice of Eastern soothsayers. Balak the king, greatly alarmed of the Israelites swarming the plains of Moab on their way from Egypt, sent for Balaam to pronounce a curse upon the people of God so that he would have nothing more to fear. Balaam refused and declared that all who blessed Israel would be blessed. Balak sent for Balaam several times tempting him with bribes which Balaam turned down. But after much pressure, he caught the bait, held out and proved he loved the wages of unrighteousness despite being forbidden by God to go to Balak. Balaam did not immediately dismiss the messengers of Balak. He asked for time to consult God what he should do even when the line of duty was already clear and there was no need to pray. God allowed Balaam to go, but did not carry divine approval with him. On his way to Balak, suddenly, the ass he was riding stopped and could not be induced to proceed. God's angel stood on his way with his drawn sword. Then the ass, the most stupid of all beasts, was made to speak and reproved Balam, who confessed: "I have sinned".

Balaam went and built seven altars and offered bullocks and rams on every altar. God was not pleased with the offering but employed Balaam for His own purposes by putting in his mouth some of the most blessed and glorious words spoken concerning His people Israel.

We should learn from Balaam that sometimes God punishes us by allowing us to have our own way. The presence of any sin is ruinous, especially covetousness, the most pious wishes are sometimes vain. The road to hell can be paved with good resolutions. To die well one must live well. The clearest knowledge without grace is worthless.

k. Jonah
Jonah was the son of Amittai, a subject of the northern kingdom, who lived in the early part of the reign of Jeroboam II when the kingdom was divided. God sent him to Nineveh beyond the boundary of Israel to warn the people against their wickedness. Jonah simply ran in the other direction, though he did not object to his call on the basis of inability, but upon the seeming irrationality of calling Nineveh to repent. Jonah saw this as an evil culture that didn't disserve a warning of impending doom. As he ran away, Jonah discovered that called ministers cannot outrun God. He was punished as he was thrown into the sea, but swallowed by a whale. He was inside the whale for three days praying and ran back to God when he was overtaken in his flight (Jonah 1: 4-17). He went back to perform the "unwelcome" task and became a revivalist (Jonah 3). Jonah was disappointed with his own work (Jon. 3:5-10; 4:1), which reveals bigotry (Jonah 4: 1-3). Jonah was

later taught the lesson of divine mercy (Jonah 4:4-11).

No one can out-run God, neither are we in position to overrule God, neither are we in position to teach God what to do. We are pencils in the hand of God, we should make ourselves available to Him so that our services can be acceptable to Him.

I. Church in Sardis

John writing for the Lord Jesus, sends messages to the seven churches including Sardis. He calls attention to something that escapes the church's attention. Sardis church – a dead church which fell asleep on the job. "**I know your works, That you have a name that you are alive, but you are dead. Be watchful, and strengthen the things which remain, that are ready to die for I have not found your works perfect before God**" (Rev. 3:1-2). The church was doing well until it fell asleep, but the message was sent to enable the church to make amends - wake up and repent - to produce acceptable service. This is a wakeup call to lukewarm and sleeping Christians to arise and repent.

CHAPTER 7

THE PURPOSE OF GRACE IN SERVICE

The purpose of grace is revealed in this phase: "**whereby we may serve God acceptably**" (Heb. 12:28).

The Greek adverb used here for "acceptably" is "euarestos", from eu (well) and arestos (pleasing). The word means well pleasing or to please well. It is used in this passage to signify, "so as to please" God. This is the function of grace; it helps us to serve God in a way that pleases Him.

The word is used of Enoch's service and walk of faith.

By faith Enoch was taken away so that he did not see death, and was not found, because God had taken him for before he was taken had this testimony, that pleased God.
(Hebrews 11:5)

Paul gave this admonition:

But do not forget to do good and to share, for with such sacrifices God is well pleased.
(Hebrews 13:16)

The adjective form of the word is used for "acceptable" in Rom. 12:1, 2.

I beseech you therefore, brethren, by the mercies of God, that you present your bodies a living sacrifice, holy, acceptable to God which is your reasonable service. And do not be conformed to this world, but be transformed by

the renewing of your mind, that you may prove what is that good and acceptable and perfect will of God. (Romans 12:1-2; see also: Rom. 14:18; Eph. 5:10).

Our desire should not only be to serve God, but to receive His grace to serve Him acceptably or "so as to please" Him. The grace of God makes our service acceptable, enjoyable and rewarding. Grace overshadows our weaknesses and "covers" us, so that we are not disgraced or put to shame.

Our service for God must be increasingly motivated by a holy desire to please God (Rom 12:1-2, Rom 6:13, 16, 19). When our works and service please the Lord, He will make even our enemies to respect us (Prov 16:7). And the more He is pleased with our service, the more He blesses and uses us. Grace is needed for these to happen.

Divine grace gives the servant the ability to serve gracefully and gratefully- not grudgingly.

Evidences of graceful service

The grace for service will reflect in the following:

***Consecration** (Rom. 12:1-2)
Consecration is the act of setting apart or dedicating something or someone for God's use. In the Old Testament, the Temple and its trappings were the most important objects consecrated to God (2 Chron. 7:5-9). Aaron and his sons were consecrated to the priesthood (Exodus 29). But even spoils of battle (Josh 6:19) and cattle could be consecrated (Lev. 27:28). First born of men and animals alike were consecrated (Exo. 13:2). The Lord Jesus Christ made

the supreme consecration of himself (John 17:19) but believers are also consecrated by Christ (John 17:17; I Pet 2:9). Believers are enjoined to consecrate themselves (Rom 12:1-2; 2 Tim 2:21). The implication of our consecration by Christ is that we are now a priesthood of believers (I Pet. 2:9) and that gives us the direct access to our heavenly Father (Eph 3:11-12). Consecration is a prerequisite for and an evidence of a graceful service.

***Joy in service**
Lost joy for soul winning can be restored (Psalm 51:12-13). Joy in service is a pointer to graceful service. For example, God loves Jesus because He fulfilled the plan of God for mankind by laying down His life for sinners (John 10:17). And the Father exalts Him above all names (Phil 2:9-11). The seventy disciples served and testified with joy. We are told: "And the seventy returned again with joy, saying, Lord, even the devils are subject unto us through thy name" (Luke 10:17 KJV).

There is also reward for the sowers and reapers who will rejoice together. The joy, therefore, of the great harvest festivity will be the common joy of all who have taken any part in the work from the first operation to the last (John 4:36). During the time of Ezra, the people wept after it was impressively brought to their remembrance by the reading of the law, they had a deep sense of national sins. But they were exhorted to cherish the feelings of joy and thankfulness associated with sacred festival of the feast of Tabernacle by sending portions of it to their poorer brethren. (See: Neh. 8:9-10).

The Psalmist writes:

Those who sow in tears shall reap in joy. He who continually goes forth weeping, bearing seed for sowing, shall doubtless come again with rejoicing bringing his sheaves with him.
(Psalm 126:5,6).

Joy will be restored to a backslidden soul won back to Christ (Psalm 51:12-13).

***Willingness to serve**
Willingness to serve is the service that comes from the heart. It is a voluntary service which is not rendered by force nor induced by any personal gain or advantage. It is a service rendered by personal conviction for the benefit of humanity to enrich the kingdom of God.

In Deborah and Barak's song of thanksgiving, after victory over Jabin, king of Canaan and Sisera his commander, they praised the Lord for the brave leadership in Israel – the people had willingly offered themselves (Judges 5:2).

Despite the vehement opposition of Sanballat to stop the rebuilding of the wall of Jerusalem by mocking, ridiculing and distracting the Jews, the work continued unhindered at an accelerated speed because "**the people had a mind to work**" (Neh. 4:6). This is a demonstration of willingness to serve. The secret of their success was unity of purpose and willingness to work. In order to promote commerce, growth and development in Jerusalem after the return from exile, the leaders of the Jews appealed to the people to dwell in Jerusalem. "**And the people blessed all men who willingly offered themselves to dwell at Jerusalem**" (Neh. 11:2; See also: 1 Chrn. 29:5-12).

God is looking for volunteers who are willing to serve in His vineyard today more than any time in history because the harvest is plenteous and the labourers are few. The Psalmist writes: "**Your people shall be volunteers in the day of your power; in the beauty of holiness, from the womb of the morning, you have the dew of your youth**" (Psalm 110:3).

In the New Life Translation, it reads: "**When you go to war, your people will serve you willingly...**". The apostles were willing to share, not only the Gospel, but their own lives, too (1 Thess. 2:8).

*Undivided loyalty
Undivided loyalty is the graceful service rendered in total commitment to God. It is a faithful service rendered to please God. It is a heart yearning to serve God by putting God and His kingdom first in everything.

When the ark of the Lord was taken away from Shiloh, over twenty years after it had remained in the home of Abinadab, the children of Israel began to revive from their sad state of religious decline. They responded wholeheartedly to Samuel's admonition to put away their foreign gods and serve only the Lord (1 Sam. 7:2-4). This is a feeling of loyalty and genuine yearning and panting of soul toward God (Psalm 42:1-2). Undivided loyalty in God's service is a key to success and divine blessing in ministry (See: Exod. 23:25; Job 36:11).

Christians are called to faithful service to God as no servant can serve two masters.

Jesus said:

No servant can serve two masters; for either he will hate the one and love the other, or else he will be loyal to the one and despise the other. You cannot serve God and mammon.
(Luke 16:13).

***Humility in service**
Humility is a mental attitude of lowliness. It is the grace developed in the Christian by the Spirit of God wherein the believer frankly acknowledges that all he has and is, he owes to God.

It is part of graceful service of ministers of God to serve with humility and not to lord it over the church as shepherds but **"to take heed to themselves and to all the flock, among which the Holy Spirit made them overseers...."** (Acts 20:28).

According to the teaching of Jesus on humility, Christians who aspire leadership positions should be ready to serve and not to be served. **"Yet it shall not be so among you, but whoever of you desires to be first shall be slave of all"** (Mark 10:43-44). Christians are enjoined to be "humble because God resists the proud but gives grace to the humble" (James 4:6). The fastest route to the top is humility. James wrote; **"Humble yourselves in the sight of the Lord, and He will lift you up"** (James 4:10).

*Grace to finish assignments
While it is imperative to embark on our assignments as believers but it is more auspicious to finish well. It

is at the end of an assignment a proper valuation can be placed on what had been accomplished. A verdict could be reached after proper valuation of the result – brilliant success, average or failure. It is not enough to embark on an assignment but to finish it well. Our reward is based on the outcome of our output, that is, our ability to finish well.

Jesus, our Saviour, is called Author and Finisher because what He started by His incarnation, He finished it at Calvary by paying the supreme price for our sin (John 19:30). He made it His priority to please and do the will of the Father during His earthly ministry (John 4:34; 8:29). In his valedictory testimony, Paul said: "**I have fought the good fight, I have finished the race, I have kept the faith**" (2 Tim 4:7). Paul saw life as a race to be won, a battle to be fought, and a trust to be kept. This is how Christians should see the challenge of our service to God.

When God calls men to serve, He gives them the grace to finish their tasks (Zech. 4:9). Indeed, He is able to finish, through His grace, whatever He has started through us, as long as we submit to His will (Phil. 1:6). Our goal should not only be to start, but to finish with joy (Acts 20:24).

*Team spirit in service
Team spirit is the spirit of working together severally and jointly to achieve our given assignment or a common goal. When there is team spirit and cooperation there is bound to be great accomplishment. The Scripture assured: "how could one chase a thousand and two put ten thousand to flight …" (Deut. 32:30).

The Psalmist, writing on blessed unity of the people of God, said: "**Behold how good and how pleasant it is for brethren to dwell together in unity. It is like the precious oil upon the head, running down on the beard, the beard of Aaron, running down on the edge of his garments**" (Psalm 133:1-2). There is a great reward for friendship or partnership because partners accomplish more and complement each other. Two are always better than one, and a friend sharpens a friend, as iron sharpens iron (Prov. 27:17).

Solomon writes:

Two are more than one, because they have a good reward for their labour. For if they fall, one will lift up his companion, but woe to him who is alone when he falls, for he has no one to help him up. Again if two lie down together, they will keep warm; but how can one be warm alone? Though one may be overpowered by another, two can withstand him. And a threefold cord is not quickly broken.
(Ecclesiastes 4: 9-12)

Paul painted the picture of the church working together as a family for the purpose of growing to maturity and fruitfulness in I Cor. 3:6-9. When we work together in the church as faithful members contributing our quota in evangelism and in our various departments – choir, prayer fellowship, Sunday school teacher, ushers etc, the church will grow in leaps and bounds.

Where Christians live and work "together in unity", the grace of God is evident among them. Graceful workers encourage unity, but graceless workers promote schism and unholy independence.

*Diligence in service

Christians are enjoined to work hard not as men pleasers but as servants working for God. In addition to your brotherly love and mutual respect to one another, Paul exhorted Christians; "not to lag in diligence, fervent spirit, serving the Lord" (Rom. 12:11). God is the Rewarder of diligent seekers (Heb. 11:6) and diligent servants (Exod. 23:25; Matt. 25:16-17, 20-23).

Therefore graceful service entails not only commitment and loyalty but also hard work, putting up our best with a view to pleasing the Master, Jesus. Those who serve diligently shall be handsomely rewarded: **"they will stand before kings, they will not stand before unknown men"** (Prov. 22:29).

*Self sacrifice

Self sacrifice is when a person willingly offers himself for the service of God. It is a total surrender for divine service without looking back, with readiness to obey and carry out His instructions. Divine grace is manifested in self sacrifice (2 Cor. 8:9). Self sacrifice is like a soldier who does not entangle himself with the affairs of this world but is fully committed to divine service. This is a model of Jesus **"who made Himself of no reputation, taking the form of a bondservant, and coming in the likeness of man"**. Paul exhorts: **"Let each of you look out not only for his own interests, but also for the interests of others"** (Phil. 2:4).

Self sacrifice enables us to overcome selfishness and self centeredness to live wholly for Christ and love others. It is the secret of fulfillment and joy in service. Sacrificing to help and build the faith of others brings a joyful reward (See: Phil. 2:17-18).

***Reverence in service** (Heb. 12:28)
Reverence in service means serving with humility, putting God first in everything we do in the service of the Lord. When we are used as a channel of blessing to others or to the church, we should let God take the glory. He will not share His glory with any one (Isa. 48; 11). When we would have done everything, we should only see ourselves as unprofitable servants. "**We have done what was our duty to do**" (Luke 17:10). Since you are not working for earthly reward that perishes, you should serve with reverence and wait for your reward. Paul writes: "**Therefore, since we are receiving a kingdom which cannot be shaken, let us have grace, by which we may serve God acceptably with reverence and godly fear**" Heb. 12:28).

***Serving in spirit and truth**
The flesh always works contrary to the Spirit, the flesh is weak, materialistic and does not think about things of God. The Spirit connects us with God; He leads and guides us against mistake and spirit of error. He is our teacher, and reminds us of what we have learnt (John 14:26, 15:26). This is why the scripture says: "**For as many as are led by the Spirit of God, these are sons of God**" (Rom. 8:14).

Jesus declared: "**God is Spirit, and those who worship Him must worship in spirit and truth**" (John 4:24). True Christians "**are the circumcision,**

who worship God in the Spirit, rejoice in Christ Jesus, and have no confidence in the flesh" (Phil. 3:3). To encounter graceful service we must serve God in spirit and truth. For our service to be rewarded we must serve God in spirit and in truth.

Grace and truth are inseparable; where there is grace, truth will be manifested (John 1:14,17; Col. 1:6). Serving in spirit and in truth is a virtue which is reflected in graceful workers.

*Submission to leadership
It is mandatory for believers to obey and submit to leaders in the church and civil authority because they are representatives of God (Rom. 13; 1-7). When you disobey the civil or church authority you disobey God. Paul, writing to younger people, said: "**submit yourselves to your elders**". Yes, all of you be submissive to one another, and be clothed with humility, for, "**God resists the proud, but gives grace to the humble. Therefore humble yourselves under the mighty hand of God, that He may exalt you in due time**" (I Peter 5:5, 6). Paul enjoined Christians "**to obey those who rule over you, and be submissive, for they watch out for your souls as those who must give account...**" (Heb. 13:17).

A rebellion against leadership is rebellion against God, therefore repent from every spirit of rebellion or disobedience so that your service will be acceptable to God.

Examples of grace in service

Examples abound in the Bible – both in the Old Testament and in the New Testament. But I will discuss only a few, due to space and time constraint.

a. Enoch
Enoch, a son of Jared, a descendant of Seth and father of Methuselah, was a man who had favour with God (Gen. 5:18-23). Though his biography was set out in only six verses but two things of great interest characterize him: (i). His holy life on earth and (ii). His glorious exit from the earth. While it is always stated in the Bible that the wicked is without God, but Enoch walked with God. Enoch was at peace with God, because two cannot walk together unless they be agreed (Amos 3:3).

Enoch enjoyed close communion with God, for him to have walked with God means there was no cloud between their fellowship. For Enoch to have walked with God it means he was separated from the world, because "friendship with the world is enmity with God" (James 4:4). Enoch's graceful service was acceptable to God, "by faith Enoch was taken away so that he did not see death, "and was not found, because God has taken him," for before he was taken he had this testimony; that he pleased God" (Heb. 11:5; Gen. 5:23, 24).

b. Joseph
Joseph was obedient to his father and loved God from his childhood. His brothers envied him and sold him to slavery in order to counter his dream. In slavery, he found the favour of his master, Potiphar, and God prospered everything entrusted to him and

he was made the overseer of Potiphar's house. As a true representative of God, he refused to compromise his integrity; he refused to be lured to sexual sin by Mrs. Potiphar, for which he was sent to prison. From prison, God elevated him to the position of a Governor in Egypt, where his dream was fulfilled, his brothers bowed down to him when they came to Egypt to purchase food. Joseph forgave his brothers; he brought the whole family to Egypt where he cared for them throughout his life time. He saw God's purpose in what happened to him (Gen. 45:50:20). Instead of vengeance, Joseph showed kindness to his brethren (Rom. 14:19; 12; 19).

c. Moses
Moses was born in Egypt at a time Pharaoh gave instruction that Hebrew male infants should be killed. But by divine arrangement, Pharaoh's Princess adopted Moses and brought him up as her son. Moses was trained as a builder and in the arts and culture of Egypt. When he grew up, he refused to be called a prince of Pharaoh but identified with Hebrew slaves. For his overzealousness, he killed an Egyptian which led to his exile in Midian for 40years, where God called him out to lead Israel out of Egypt. Moses was the meekest man on earth and faithful in all the house of God (Acts 7:21, 22). Moses made the right choice by aligning with his people who were slaves in Egypt rather than being called a prince. His humble service of writing the first five books of the Bible and giving the law to his people have impacted both the Old Testament and New Testament believers. He rendered selfless service, a great intercessor who refused to take undue advantage over his erring brethren. (Exo. 32: 9-14). He is regarded as one of the greatest and most influential

Prophets in the Bible because he rendered graceful service to God and humans.

d. Joshua and Caleb
Joshua and Caleb were among the twelve people chosen from each tribe sent by Moses to spy out the land of Canaan. On their return, both men gave positive minority report believing that God would possess the land for Israel. But the ten spies agreed that the land was flowing with milk and honey but that giants, descendants of Anak, inhabited the land, that the land devoured the inhabitants while the children of Israel were like grasshoppers. It was the evil report which the people believed that led to God's pronouncement of death on the adults up to the age of twenty; He also extended the journey from 40 days to 40 years. God promised blessings upon Joshua and Caleb for their loyalty and faith (Num. 14: 29, 30).

Eventually, Joshua the servant of Moses, became the successor of Moses (Num. 27: 18-23). He eventually shared the land for all the tribes and Caleb. Israel served the Lord during the life time of Joshua and he challenged them to be loyal to God before he died (Joshua 24: 15). Both men were loyal and faithful to God and rendered graceful service and they fought on the side of the people to deliver the land of Canaan from the inhabitants of the land.

e. Nehemiah
Nehemiah was one of the captives brought to Babylon who served as a cup-bearer for King Artaxerxes. He was a contemporary of Ezra. One day, Nehemiah heard that the walls surrounding Jerusalem lay in ruins, a disgrace to Hebrews.

Nehemiah wept, saw a need, prayed, rose up, captured a vision, laid a plan and mobilized others to join him in his cause. Despite opposition, from Sanbalat and others, Nehemiah mobilized and inspired the people to build the wall of Jerusalem which was completed in 52 days (Neh. 6: 15). He eventually became the Governor and he was a model of a selfless leader who waived his entitlements and did not ask for any reward (Neh. 5: 14-15). He served his people without asking to be served, the model advocated by the Lord Jesus in Mark 10: 42-45. This is the graceful service God expects from leaders either in the Church or in civil government.

f. Apostle Paul
Paul was born a Jew, from the tribe of Benjamin, a Sanhedrin who was under the tutelage of Gamaliel. He was very zealous for Judaism; he persecuted, arrested and imprisoned Christians, followers of the Lord Jesus Christ. On a glorious day, on his way to Damascus, Syria, to arrest and imprison disciples, he was arrested by the Lord Jesus Christ (Acts 9: 1-9). He later joined the Church in Antioch where "the Spirit separated Paul and Barnabas apart" as missionaries to the Gentiles.

Paul brought the same zeal he had for Judaism to his work as a missionary to the Gentiles. He suffered persecution, hunger, shipwreck and imprisonment for preaching the gospel of Jesus Christ. The Lord used him to write half of the New Testament books. Paul lived a selfless life, a life of commitment to the cause of the gospel and the Lord Jesus Christ, and was a loyal servant of the God who used him mightily and exposed him to many revelations. He worked harder and accomplished great exploits beyond his peers, because of the grace of God upon him.

Jesus: our perfect example

Jesus Christ, the Son of God, was born of a Virgin, named Mary, according to the plan of God to redeem mankind from sin (Isa. 7: 14; Rom. 7: 17). At the age of 12, He was found in the "Temple among scholars, both listening to them and asking them questions. And Jesus increased in wisdom and stature, and in favour with God and men" (Luke 2: 46, 52).

When He was 30 years old, He began His ministry in earnest and chose twelve disciples to follow and remain with Him. He reproduced Himself in them. Jesus is the embodiment of loyalty, love, commitment and sacrificial service.

Jesus said: "My food is to do the will of Him that sent Me and to finish His work" (John 4: 34). In everything, Christ showed us a model of integrity, selfless service and His priority was always to please the Father (John 8: 29). Just as through Adam sin and death passed to the human race, so through the obedience and death of Jesus Christ, we have abundant grace for remission of sin (Rom. 5:14-17). He died and rose from the dead for our justification so that we can become the righteousness of God (II Cor. 5: 21). He manifested His generous grace in His self sacrifice. Though He was rich, yet He became poor for our sakes, so that He could make us rich by His poverty (2 Cor. 8:9). He ascended to heaven to prepare a place for us (John 14: 3). Today, He is our intercessor before the Father and He is able to preserve us until He returns to take the saints home (Heb. 7: 25). What a Mighty God we serve!

The servants with five and one talents

The parable of the talents in Matthew 25 fully illustrates acceptable, consecrated and rewarding service on the one hand and unacceptable service actuated by presumptuous spirit, self pleasing attitude and lack of consecration on the other hand. The first servant was given five talents by the Master before he embarked on a journey to a far country. The second servant was given two talents while the third servant was given one talent; "to each according to his own ability" (Matt. 25: 14-15).

On his return, the Master asked for account of stewardship from each servant. The first servant reported a gain of five talents on the five talents given to him, while the third servant buried his talent instead of working with it. He said to his Lord: "I know you to be a hard man, reaping from where you have not sown and gathering where you have not scattered. And I was afraid and went and hid your talent in the ground. Look there you have what is yours" (Matt. 25: 24-25). While the other two servants were handsomely rewarded for their faithful service, the third, lazy, wicked and unprofitable servant, was cast into outer darkness and his talent was given to the first servant who made a profit of five talents. This is how every service will be rewarded at the last day-reward of heaven for faithful and righteous servants (Matt. 25: 20-23) and outer darkness for the unrighteous and unfaithful servants (Matt. 25: 26-30).

CHAPTER 8

STANDING GRACE

Standing grace or grace for standing is the grace by which we are kept from falling or failing. It is the grace we need to stand in faith, in holiness and in battle. With this grace we stand, but fall in disgrace without grace. The God who saved us by His grace is "able to keep us from falling" (Jude 24), by the same grace. Divine grace is sufficiently strong to make us strong (2 Tim. 2:1), strengthened (2 Cor. 12: 9-10) and to stand (Rom. 5:2). It is not by our power that we are still standing in the faith while others have fallen (Zech. 4:6; I Sam. 2:9); but it is by the special grace of God. Divine grace therefore, is indispensable in Christian standing.

Men fall without Grace

We are liable to fail or fall without God's grace sustaining us. Strong and mighty men are falling because of lack of grace.

Even the youth shall faint and be weary, and the young men shall utterly fall. But those who wait on the Lord shall renew their strength; they shall mount up with wings like eagles, they shall run and not be weary, they shall walk and not faint.

(Isaiah 40:30,31).

Without God's grace we can fall into sin, into temptation, fall into reproach and condemnation (2 Tim. 3:6-7), fall under pressure, fall in battle. It is presumptuous to think that we can stand without grace. Paul warns: **"Therefore let him that**

thinketh he standeth take heed lest he fall" (1 Cor. 10:12 KJV)

The Bible states that **"where no counsel is the people fall" (Prov. 11:14)** and "where there is no vision, the people perish" (Prov. 29:18). We may well substitute "counsel" and "vision" with "grace". Thus, we can say, **"where there is no grace, the people fall"**. Trusting in our riches instead of trusting God's grace will lead to failure. (Prov. 11:28).

Saul fell disgracefully and dishonourably in battle because he lost God's favour in his life. His fall began when he began to disobey God (I Sam. 15: 22-23). And, gradually, as he sank lower in "disgrace", he lost God's favour.

And having no grace or favour with God, Saul sought help from the witch of Endor (I Sam. 28). Saul was an embarrassment to his high position as a king and even to God who appointed him. He was rebellious, disobedient and envious of David after killing Goliath. He hated David and did everything in his power to kill him. When Saul could no longer hear from the Lord, he went to the witch of Endor for divination on the eve of his battle with the Philistines. Eventually, Saul died in the battle against the Philistines. He actually committed suicide. The Bible states:

"Now the Philistines fought against Israel, and the men of Israel fled from before the Philistines, and fell slain on Mount Gibeon. Then the Philistines followed hard after Saul and his sons. And the Philistines killed Jonathan, Abinadab, and Malchishua, Saul's sons. The battle became fierce against Saul.

The archers hit him, and he was severely wounded by the archers. Then Saul said to his armour bearer, "Draw your sword, and thrust me through with it, lest these uncircumcised men come and thrust me through and abuse me". But his armour bearer would not, for he was greatly afraid. Therefore Saul took a sword and fell on it. And when his armour bearer saw that Saul was dead, he also fell on his sword, and died with him. So Saul, his three sons, his armour bearer, all his men died together that same day."

(I Sam. 31: 1-6).

David composed this song to mourn Saul's death:

"The beauty of Israel is slain on your high places! How the mighty have fallen! Tell it not in Gath, proclaim it not in the streets of Ashkelon – lest the daughters of Philistines rejoice, lest the daughters of the uncircumcised triumph...How the mighty have fallen in the midst of the battle Jonathan was slain in your high places....."How the mighty have fallen, And the weapons of war perishes".

(2 Sam. 1: 19-20, 25, 27).

Once a Christian falls from grace, he loses favour with God, disgrace and shame begins to stare him in the face.

By Grace We Stand

Grace provides the "**good ground**" (See Matt. 13: 8; Mark 4:8; Luke 8:8), the solid ground or solid rock, upon which we stand "**rooted and grounded**" (Eph. 3: 17), "**grounded and settled**" and not easily "**moved away from the hope of the gospel**" (Col. 1: 23). Even in our seemingly weak conditions, God can uphold us and lift us up, when we fall – all because of His grace.

When our course of life is pleasing to God, He will order our way, failures will not be permanent. The Psalmist writes. "**The steps of a good man are ordered by the Lord, and He delights in his way. Though he falls, he shall not be utterly cast down for the Lord upholds him with His hand**" (Psalm 37: 23 – 24).

It takes the grace of God for Christians to overcome challenges and stand firm in the Lord. According to the Psalmist: "**The Lord upholds all who fall, and raises up all who are bowed down**" (Psalm 145: 14).

Comparing the righteous and the wicked, Solomon asserts: "**For a righteous man may fall seven times and arise again but the wicked shall fall by calamity**" (Prov. 24: 16). God Himself is the strength and succour to the righteous, always ready to lift them up and keep them from falling.

The Parable of the wise and foolish builders perfectly illustrates this truth. Jesus said:

Therefore whoever hears these saying of Mine, and does them, I will liken him to a wise man who built his house on the rock and the rain descended, the floods came, and the winds blew and beat on that house; and it did not fall, for it was founded on the rock. But everyone who hears these sayings of Mine, and does not do them, will be like a foolish man who built his

house on the sand and the rain descended, and floods came, and the winds blew and beat on that house and it fell, and great was its fall.
(Matt. 7: 24 – 27).

In this parable, the wise builder can be described as a Christian who builds on God's grace; a graceful Christian builds on Christ, the Solid Rock. We are told that:

And the rain descended, the floods came, and the wind blew and beat on that house, and it did not fall, for it was founded on the rock.
(Matt. 7: 25)

He is like a man building a house, who dug deep and laid the foundation on the rock. And the flood arose, the stream beat vehemently against that house, and could not shake it, for it was founded on the rock.
(Luke 6: 48)

And, consequently, inspite of his trials and challenges "**it fell not for it was founded upon a rock**". (Matt. 7: 25), "**and could not shake it: for it was founded upon a rock** "(Luke 6: 48).

The foolish man, however, is a graceless builder who builds without grace; he trusts in his own natural abilities, instead of trusting God's grace. We are told:

"But everyone who hears these sayings of Mine, and does not do them, will be like a foolish man who built his house on the sand and the rain descended, the floods came, and the winds blew and beat on that house; and it fell. And great was its fall." (Matt. 7: 26 -27).

But he who heard and did nothing is **"like a man who built a house on the earth without a foundation, against which the stream beat vehemently. And immediately and it fell; and the ruin of that house was great,"** (Luke 6: 49).

The foolish man's house falls under pressure, trials and crises. We are told, and **"it fell; and great was the fall of it" (Matt. 7: 27),** "and immediately it fell; and the ruin of that house was great" (Luke 6: 49).

To stand means: get to your feet, rise, stand up, straighten up, pick yourself up, find your feet. The Dictionary defines the verb "stand" as: to be upright, be erect, be vertical, be on your feet. The word "stand" also connotes; to be upright, to stand erect, to be firm-unmovable, undefeated, to endure, to be successful, to win, to win a battle or survive a storm.

Paul wrote the Christians in Ephesus on the need to "stand" in the midst of battle and satanic attack.

Put on the whole armour of God that you may be able to stand against the wiles of the devil... Therefore, take up the whole armour of God that you may be able to withstand in the evil day, and having done all, to stand. Stand therefore, having guarded your waist with truth, having put on the breastplate of righteousness.
                    (Ephesians 6: 11, 13, 14).

Paul used the word "stand" and "withstanding" to emphasize the need to stand; not just standing, but standing firm, standing strong, standing against the enemy both during a battle and after a battle.

Paul also admonished us to:
a. Stand in the Gospel of faith (I Cor. 15: 1)
b. Stand fast in faith (I Cor. 16: 13)
c. Stand fast in the liberty of Christ (Gal. 5: 1)
d. Stand fast in the Spirit (Phil. 1: 27)
e. Stand fast in the Lord (Phil. 4: 1)
f. Stand perfect and complete in all the will of God (Col. 4: 12).

Standing on Grace

Paul wrote to the Church in Rome:

Therefore, having been justified by faith we have peace with God through our Lord Jesus Christ, through whom also we have access by faith into grace in which we stand and rejoice in hope of the glory of God.
(Rom. 5:1-2)

According to Paul, we stand on grace or in favour in relation to God. We stand justified not condemned before God, on the ground of grace. Grace puts us in a favourable position with God. Thus, we enjoy the blessings of justified life, as we stand on grace; these include access by faith into divine favour and joy in the hope of the glory of God.

Our faith in Christ Jesus earns us peace with God and we are translated into permanent standing in favour with God which the justified enjoy (Rom. 5: 2 – 3).

The Greek word used in Rom. 5: 2 for "stand" is "histemi", which denotes to stand, to continue, to abide, to hold up, to stand still. Thus, through this grace, we can stand strong, stand firm, stand up and stand boldly. The same word is used for standing on the true grace, in I Pet. 5: 12: "**By Silvanus, our faithful brother as I consider him, I have written to you briefly, exhorting and testifying that this is the true grace of God in which you stand.**"

This verse is directly linked with verse 10, where Peter said: "**May the God of all grace, who called us to His eternal glory of Christ Jesus, after you have suffered a while, perfect, establish, strengthen, and settle you,**" (I Pet. 5: 10).

The God of all grace – the source of grace – "who called us and started the work of grace in us, is able to help us finish what He has started" (See: Phil. 1: 6).

It is grace that is able to keep us throughout all our trials, challenges, troubles and in all our sufferings. After we have suffered for a while, God, by His grace "**will restore, support, and strengthen you and he will place you on a firm foundation**" (I Pet. 5: 10; NLT). This way, we come out better, stronger, standing, firmer, after our trials (See: I Pet. 1: 7).

Our suffering for the Gospel's sake needs further attestation and confirmation of truth which we can stand upon. And because we are standing on the "**true grace,**" our standing is true. Thus, we cannot be disappointed, defeated or fall as long as we stand on this grace.

The Purpose of Standing Grace

Grace provides us with invaluable help and strength to stand and fulfill God's purpose in our lives. Standing on grace amounts to standing with God or on God's side; and God's side is "the winning side". Grace helps us to stand in the following areas of Christian experience:

a. To stand still and see the salvation of God

The approach of the Egyptian army terrified the Israelites, and they placed heavy pressure on their leader Moses to handle the crisis. Moses remained calm, since he had witnessed the miracles of God in Egypt. He exuded both poise and confidence and said to the people, "**do not be afraid. Stand still, and see the salvation of the Lord, which He will accomplish for you today**" (Exo. 14: 13).

When a great army of Moabites, Ammorites and others which outnumbered the forces of Judah stared destruction in the face of Jehoshaphat, God spoke through Jahaziel to allay their fear: "**You will not need to fight in this battle, position yourselves, stand still and see the salvation of the Lord, who is with you O Judah and Jerusalem! Do not fear or be dismayed; tomorrow go out against them, for the Lord is with you**" (2 Chro. 20: 17). In time of crises Christians should not panic but have confidence in the Lord who is always ready to miraculously deliver His people.

b. To stand in awe and sin not

Christians are enjoined to exalt and honour God because those who honour Him, He will honour. We are also enjoined to control our emotions and put our anger in check even in the height of provocation.

The Psalmist writes: "**Be angry, and do not sin. Meditate within your heart on your bed, and be still**" (Psalm 4: 4). Ephesians 4: 26 gives the same injunction, "**be angry and do not sin,**" and adds; "**do not let sin go down on your wrath**".

c. To stand when everyone else is falling
We have the most comforting assurance of God's protection in Psalm 91. It describes the security believers can enjoy through faith in the Lord. The Lord is our strength, refuge and strong tower, consequently our safety is guaranteed. "**A thousand may fall at your side, and ten thousand at your right hand; but it shall not come near you**" (Psalm 91: 7).

d. To continue standing in the old path
Christianity is often referred to as the "old way" or the "old rugged cross" to distinguish it from other religions and a modern degeneracy from good. Speaking through Prophet Jeremiah, God warned Judah against forsaking God: "**Stand in the ways and see, and ask for the old paths, where the good way is, and walk in it; then you will find rest for your souls. But they said, we will not walk in**" (Jer. 6: 16). It is always disastrous for anyone or a group of people to separate themselves from God. The recalcitrance of the Jews eventually led them into 70years slavery in Babylon according to the prophecy of Jeremiah (Jeremiah 25: 11). It is in your interest to walk and stand in the old way so that it can be well with you (Isa. 3: 10).

e. To stand perfect in God's will
To stand perfect in God's will means doing the perfect will of God in our daily lives in order to please Him. The scripture enjoins Christians "to be perfect

as our heavenly Father is perfect" (Matt. 5: 48). In his letter to the Colossian Church, Paul referred to Epaphras as one who "**was always labouring fervently for the church in prayers that they may stand perfect and complete in all the will of God**" (Colossians 4: 12).

f. To stand at the liberty provided by Christ
Every born again Christian has been set free from the bondage of sin and the grand deception of the devil. As many as are set free by Jesus who took our sins away on the cross are free indeed (John 8: 32, 36). Paul admonished the Galatian church "**to stand therefore in the liberty by which Christ has made us free, and do not be entangled again with a yoke of bondage**" (Gal. 5: 1). This is a warning to believers not to go back to sin from which they have been saved and set free by the Lord Jesus Christ.

g. To stand alone with God
Paul, the apostle to the Gentiles was courageous and knew how to endure persecution. He also taught Timothy, his spiritual son the process of taking a stand in many tough situations. During his incarceration, he was forsaken by his associates and admirers but he stood with God. Paul writes: "**At my first defense no one stood with me, but all forsook me. May it not be charged against them. But the Lord stood with me and strengthened me, so that the message might be preached fully through me, and that all the Gentiles might hear. Also I was delivered out of the mouth of the Lion**" (2 Tim.4: 16-17). The lesson from Paul's predicament is that when friends and everyone else forsake us God will never forsake us. God is the only true friend in times of challenges.

h. To stand the storms of life
There are storms of life like; sickness, challenges of joblessness, death of a loved one, inability to settle one's bills, natural **disasters such as flooding and hurricane. Jesus said: "These things I have spoken to you, that in Me you have peace. In the world you will have tribulation but be of good cheer, I have overcome the world**" (John 16: 33). Our anchor as Christians is Jesus, our Saviour, Redeemer and Provider. He is the only rock we can build on, that can withstand the storms of life, rain, flood or wind (Matt. 7: 25). The Lord is our Refuge in the time of storm. Therefore, if you trust Him, He will cause your wars to cease and calm every storm in your life (Psalm 46: 1 – 10; Mark 4: 35- 41).

i. Stand against satanic attack
The scripture enjoins believers to "be sober, be vigilant, because your adversary the devil walks about like a roaring lion seeking whom he may devour "(I Pet. 5: 8). Satan is our enemy, we must be vigilant and ready to resist him at all times because it is dangerous to give him a chance. To withstand him effectively we must "put on the whole armour of God, that you may be able to stand against the wiles of the devil" (Eph. 6: 11).

j. To stand in the time of evil
Satan is the author of evil, promoting and spreading sin all over the world – pornography, sodomy, same sex marriage, internet scam, etc. In this end time, we are living in evil days, perilous times of multiplier effect of sin especially among the youths. For believers to overcome the time of evil, we must **"take up the whole armour of God, that you**

may be able to withstand in the evil day and having done all, to stand**" (Eph. 6: 13). We must live righteously, contend for our faith, resist the devil with the word of God and prayer. I urge you to remember your creator in your youth, "while the evil days come not (Eccl. 12: 1), so that He might remember and give you grace to stand in the time of evil. (Psalm 27: 5).

k. To stand firm against sin and temptation
The Devil tempts every believer. He tempted Job and our Lord Jesus Christ (Job. 1: 8 – 19; Matt. 4: 1 – 10). The sources of temptation are: lusts, enticement and sin. James wrote: **"Let no one say when he is tempted, "I am tempted of God…But each one is tempted when he is drawn away by his own desires and enticed. Then when desire has conceived, it gives birth to sin: and sin, when it is full – grown brings forth death**" (Jam. 1: 13 – 15). While anyone can be tempted, but yielding to temptation is sin. Joseph was tempted by Mrs. Potiphar but Joseph resisted the temptation and fled (Gen. 39:9 – 12). Therefore, resist the devil and he will flee from you (Jam. 4: 7).

l. To keep standing in holiness
Holiness means sanctity, sacredness, purity, divinity, righteousness, piety, godliness and for this reason the scripture admonish Christians "to pursue peace with all people, and holiness without which no one can see God". (Heb. 12: 14). The attributes of God include purity, divinity and holiness, therefore, we should be holy as our Father (I Pet. 1: 15: 16) and without holiness no one can see God and no worship service will be acceptable to Him. Consequently, there will be no reward for unacceptable service, which amounts to effort in futility.

m. To walk worthy of our calling
Paul enjoined the Ephesian Church to walk in newness of life according to their calling of grace from darkness into the Lord's marvelous light Eph. 4: 1- 3). Christians should therefore abase themselves in the spirit in which they accept God's dealings of mercy by saving them from perdition. We should not abuse the work of grace but, as His handiwork created for good works, we should manifest His marvelous light through our good works (Matt. 5: 16).

n. To remain steadfast and unmovable
We need to summon courage to fire up our convictions to stay on, and fulfill our mission as believers. Though there are many challenges facing Christians, but we should not allow them to weigh us down, discourage or pressurize us to give up. There is victory ahead if we persevere.

Paul writes: "**Therefore, my beloved brethren, be steadfast, immovable, always, abounding in the work of the Lord, knowing that your labour is not in vain in the Lord**" (I Cor. 15: 58). Peter reminds us of the activities of the devil which is inimical to positive development and growth of Christians all over the world and has charged us to resist him. "**Resist him, steadfast in the faith, knowing that the same sufferings are experienced by your brotherhood in the world**" (I Pet. 5: 9).

Finally, we have the onerous task to resist the temptation and allurements of Satan to come out clean and finish well our Christian race. Follow this admonition of Peter: "**You therefore beloved, since you know this beforehand beware lest you also fall from your own steadfastness, being led away with the error of the wicked; but grow in grace and knowledge of our Lord and saviour Jesus Christ** (2 Pet. 3: 17 – 18).

CHAPTER 9

FALLING FROM GRACE

Can a true Christian fall from grace? Can a true believer backslide and be lost in eternity? A true believer – saved by grace – who continues in grace and grows steadily in grace and holiness, will not fall or be lost; for God is able to "keep him from falling" (Jude 24) and keep him saved "to the uttermost" (Heb. 7:25). But a believer who presumptuously abuses the grace of God and fails to repent can be lost in eternity – if he dies in sin.

The possibility of a Christian "falling from grace" is a theological controversy which has resulted to two differing schools of thought, each maintaining an extreme view. These are: Calvinism and Arminianism.

Calvinism teaches the doctrine of "once saved, always saved" and "eternal security". That is, a Christian can never be lost; that his eternal security is guaranteed; that even if he backslides, God will divinely make a way for his restoration. Thus, a Christian cannot fall from grace and end up in eternal Hell.

The Arminians do not agree with the Calvinists; they believe in the possibility of falling from grace; that Divine grace can be abused and lost; thus a believer can fall from grace.

The Calvinists and Arminians represent two extreme views of Divine grace, though both have scriptural references to support their theology. While the Calvinists believe that God is the ultimate, the Arminians stress the human part that man is responsible.

Most Evangelical scholars maintain a middle position, which is a balanced theology. While God's saving grace is entirely free – unearned and unmerited – we must cooperate with God and make use of the means of grace to remain saved and ultimately enjoy the eternal blessings of salvation.

Writing to the Philippian church, Paul admonished them "to work out your own salvation" the more carefully especially in his absence. Paul reminded them not to think the work of salvation cannot go on because he was absent (Phil 2:12). Salvation is worked in believers (vs.13) by the Spirit who enables them through faith to be justified once for all; but it needs, as a progressive work, to be worked out by obedience through the help of the same Spirit unto perfection.

Fruitful growth in faith does not happen in a day, but it is a daily process. Peter listed some characteristics of the process in 2 Pet. 1:5-7, which include: faith, virtue, discipline, knowledge, self-control, perseverance, godliness, brotherly kindness and love. Peter concluded:

Therefore, brethren, be even more diligent to make your call and election sure, for if you do these things, you will never stumble.
(2 Pet. 1:10)

Therefore beloved, looking forward to those things, be diligent to be found by Him in peace, without spot and blameless.
(2 Pet. 3:14)

Falling from Grace

It is possible for a Christian to "fall from grace" and be lost, except he repents. Salvation is by Divine grace alone, but this grace can be abused and rendered ineffective through sin.

The Bible warns:

Therefore we must give the more earnest heed to the things we have heard, lest we drift away. For if the word spoken through angels proved steadfast, and every transgression and disobedience received a just reward, how shall we escape if we neglect so great a salvation, which at the first began to be spoken by the Lord, and was confirmed to us by those who heard Him.

(Hebrews 2:1-3)

The fall of Lucifer who later became Satan, clearly shows that one can fall from grace. Before his fall, Lucifer was an archangel, the anointed cherub (Ezek 28:14), who guarded the holiness of God. But he became proud, rebellious and abused his privileges; thus, he "**fell from grace**". His fall is recorded by Isaiah:

How you are fallen from heaven, o Lucifer, son of the morning! How you are cut down to the ground, You who weakened the nations! For you have said in your heart 'I will ascend into heaven, I will exalt my throne above the stars of God; I will also sit on the mount of the congregation on the farthest sides of the north; I will ascend above the heights of the clouds, I will be like the Most High.

(Isaiah 14:12-14)

The story of Lucifer's fall is a strong warning to every Christian. We should not take God's grace for granted. "**Let him that thinketh he stands take heed lest he falls** "(I Cor. 10:12). Moreover, we should not continue consciously in sin and treat God's grace with levity.

What shall we say then? Shall we continue in sin, that grace may abound?
(Rom.6: 1)

There is a difference however, between fallen angels and fallen saints; while satan and his angels are destined for eternal Hell (Matt. 25: 41), backsliding Christians who genuinely repent and return to God can be forgiven and restored. (2 Chro. 7: 14; I John 1; 7-9).

The risen Lord gave this admonition to the Church of Ephesus:

Nevertheless I have this against you, that you have left your first love. Remember therefore from where you have fallen: repent and do the first works, or else I will come to you quickly and remove your lampstand from its place – unless you repent.
(Rev. 2: 4-5)

The Scriptural Basis

The expression "falling from grace" is based on the following scriptures:

a.) Paul wrote to the Galatians: "**Christ is become of no effect unto you, whosoever of you are**

justified by law; ye are fallen from grace"(Gal. 5: 4)

The Greek verb used here for "fallen" is "expipto", which means to fall out, to drop away, to be driven out of one's course. Paul used the word to reprimand the Christians in Galatia for reversion to Judaism and seeking to be justified by the Law, instead of walking in the grace of God. To them, Paul said, "**Ye are fallen away from grace**". The word is also used by Peter to warn believers against falling away from the course which they have been confirmed by the word of the Lord.

"**You therefore, beloved, since you know this beforehand, beware lest you also fall from your own steadfastness, being led away by the error of the wicked**".
(2 Pet. 3: 17)

The same word is used in the Apocalypse to describe the apostate condition of the church in Ephesus.

"**Remember therefore from where you have fallen; repent and do the first works, or else I will come to you quickly and remove your lampstand from its place – unless you repent**".
(Rev. 2: 5)

The Greek word (expipto) is from another Greek word "pipto", which denotes to fall down, to fail. It is translated "fall" in reference to persons who have fallen morally or spiritually.

Nor let us commit sexual immorality, as some of them did, and in one day twenty-three

thousand fell. Therefore let him who thinks he stands take heed lest he falls.

(I Cor. 10: 8, 12)

b.) In Hebrew 12:15, Paul speaks of those who "fail" where the grace of God is concerned. The apostles warns against the poisonous root of bitterness which might defile a Christian and cause him to "fail" or "fall" from grace.

Looking carefully lest anyone fall short of the grace of God; lest any root of bitterness spring up cause trouble, and by this many become defiled.

(Heb. 12: 15)

Paul used the Greek word "hustereo" for "fail" which denotes to be inferior, to fall short, to be destitute, to become worse. The word is used for "come short", in these scriptures:

For all have sinned and fall short of the glory of God.

(Rom. 3: 23)

Therefore, since a promise remains of entering His rest, let us fear lest any of you seem to have come short of it.

(Heb. 4: 1)

c.) **End time apostasy**
In Paul's letter to the Thessalonians, he predicted the apostasy of the last days which will precede the second coming of Christ and the Antichrist.

Let no man deceive you by any means; for that day shall not come, except there come a falling

away first, that man of sin be revealed, the son of perdition.

(2 Thess. 2: 3 KJV)

The Greek word "apostasia" is used here for "falling away", which also denotes defection from truth and apostasy. The "apostasy" is in reference to the faith or the biblical standard of holiness.

Paul also wrote a similar letter to Timothy, concerning this end time apostasy.

Now the spirit expressly says that in latter times Some will depart from the faith, giving heed to deceiving spirit and doctrines of demons, speaking lies in hypocrisy, having their own conscience seared with a hot iron, forbidding to marry, and commanding to abstain from foods which God created to be received with thanksgiving by those who believe and know the truth.

(1 Tim. 4: 1-3)

Apostasy is one of the major signs of the end time (see: 2 Tim. 3: 1-8, 4: 3; etc). Many Christians will "fall from grace", fall from the truth, fall from first love, fall from the standard of holiness, fall into reproach or fall into condemnation (See: I Cor. 10: 12; Gal. 5: 4, 2 Thess. 2: 3; I Tim. 3: 6, 7; 6: 10; Heb. 4: 11; 6: 6; Jam. 5: 12; Rev. 2: 4-5).

Jesus said: **"And because lawlessness will abound, the love of many will grow cold"** (Matt. 24: 12).

Abusing Divine Grace
One major reason for "falling from grace" or backsliding is presumptuous sin, taking God's grace for granted. Divine grace can be abused and rendered ineffective and can be lost.

The following negative attitudes can render the grace of God ineffective.

a.   Continuing in sin
Salvation means redemption from sin and forgiveness of past sin. It is a new life in Christ Jesus which offers a repentant sinner the opportunity to live above sin (Rom. 6: 14). Salvation is separation from sin. Therefore, salvation and sin are mutually exclusive. A forgiven sinner cannot continue in sin because sin is incompatible with new life of holiness into which a sinner is called (Rom. 6: 12). Continuing in sin renders grace ineffective.

b.   Ignoring Divine Grace
Divine grace is free salvation offered by God through His son, Jesus Christ to sinners. Anyone who accepts the free salvation receives pardon for past sin and the assurance of eternal life. Anyone who rejects the offer does so at his/her own peril because no sinner will enter the kingdom of God. Paul warned: "**We then, as workers together with Him also plead with you not to receive the grace of God in vain**" (2 Cor. 6: 1).

c.   Neglecting one's salvation
Jesus Christ paid the supreme price, for sinners to be saved, on the cross. The free offer of forgiveness from sin is attractive enough for every sinner to

accept but neglecting it is not an option because no sinner will behold the glory of God.

Paul asked: **"How shall we escape if we neglect so great a salvation, which at first began to be spoken by the Lord, and was confirmed to us by those who heard Him**" (Heb. 2: 3).

d. Disrespecting the Spirit of Grace

In the Old Testament, apostasy answers to such an utter violation of the covenant which is punishable by death (Deut. 17: 2-7). Therefore, anyone who has received Christian experiences through the spirit that confers grace or the Jews who became Christians and reversed to Judaism, have become guilty of insulting the spirit of grace. The Galatians were particularly guilty of this error (Gal. 2: 21; 3: 3; 4: 10; 5: 2). He who does not accept the benefits conferred by the spirit of grace, which includes the blood of covenant shed by Jesus, insults Him who confers it.

Paul writes: "Of how much worse punishment, do you suppose, will he be thought worthy who has trampled the Son of God underfoot, counted the blood of the covenant by which he was sanctified a common thing, and insulted the spirit of grace? (Heb. 10: 29).

e. Bad Stewardship of Divine Grace

Spiritual gifts which are products of divine grace are intended to serve people, not bolster our reputation and every one of us has at least one spiritual gift. We must use our gifts as stewards, not owners. We lead best when we lead by using our gifts gracefully, for the glory of God and for the growth of the Church.

Peter admonishes: "**As each one has received a gift, minister it to one another, as good stewards of the manifold grace of God**" (I Pet. 4:10).

f. Divine Grace can be hindered through pride

God is the giver of all things including spiritual gifts but the moment we display pride, He removes His gifts from us. Thus, we become deprived of the privileges of divine grace.

Peter: writes: **"Likewise you young people, submit yourselves to your elders. Yes, all of you be submissive to one another, and be clothed with humility, for God resists the proud, but gives grace to the humble"** (I Pet. 5:5).

God gives grace to the humble and resists the proud (Jam. 4: 6).

g. Destroying Divine Grace

Jude, in his epistle, warned the church against seducers in doctrine and practice which leads to God's vengeance on apostates. He advocated confrontation as a necessary evil against "**ungodly men who turn the grace of our God into lewdness and deny the only Lord God and our Lord Jesus Christ**" (Jude vs. 4). The confrontation is needed in order to rectify, purify and unify the church and prevent the ungodly men from destroying Divine grace. These are men who turned the Gospel state of grace and liberty into a ground of licentiousness, as if their exemption from the law gave them a license to sin.

h. The poisonous root of bitterness

This is a root whose essence is bitterness. "**Lest there should be among you a root that beareth gall and wormwood**" (Deut. 29:18 KJV). Root of bitterness comprehends every person and every principle of doctrine or practice so radically corrupt as to spread corruption all around. Paul warned the church: "**Looking carefully lest anyone fall short of the grace of God; lest any root of bitterness springing up cause trouble, and by this many become defiled; lest there be any fornicator or profane person like Esau, who for one morsel of food sold his birthright**" (Heb. 12; 15-16).

The only safety valve is in rooting out such a root of bitterness to prevent it from spreading.

i. Carelessness and overconfidence

Paul reminds Christians to learn from the past. The first generation of the children of Israel had opportunity to enter the Promised Land (I Cor. 10: 1-5) but never made it. These things were written as example for us. "**Therefore let him who thinks he stands take heed lest he fall**" (I Cor. 10: 12). Those who trust in their "Chariots and horses" – instead of Divine grace – will be "**brought down and fallen**" (Psalm 20: 7-8). And those who trust in their own strength and resources will fall (Prov. 11: 28).

We should have confidence in the Lord instead of reposing confidence in ourselves. We are to remain teachable and learn from the past.

CHAPTER 10

PROPER ATTITUDE TO DIVINE GRACE

Although Divine grace is a free gift from God, we need to maintain the right attitude towards grace to remain saved. One may truly receive a "free gift", but it is one's responsibility to protect this gift; the receiver must consistently "maintain" this gift to keep it functional and effective. Thus, while God's grace is free, but on the part of the receiver, it must be "respected" and "properly managed".

We receive God's grace without "work" (Eph. 2: 8-9), but we "maintain" the grace by "working". Writing to the Philippian Church, Paul said: **"Therefore, my beloved, as you have always obeyed, not as in my presence only, but now much more in my absence, work your own salvation with fear and trembling"** (Philippians 2: 12).

We need to "work out" our salvation, to demonstrate the reality of our faith in God (James 2: 24- 26), our appreciation to Him for His gift and our sense of responsibility (Luke 12: 48).

To "work out" our salvation implies "diligence", we need to "work" at it, to make it work for us.

Therefore, brethren, be even more diligent to make your call and election sure, for if you do these things you will never stumble.

(2 Pet. 1: 10)

Every Christian who has been "saved by grace" should maintain the following positive and proper attitudes towards divine grace.

a. Continue in Grace

It only stands to reason to continue in grace that saves us and perfects the work of grace in us because it is only those who endure to the end that will be saved. Paul and Barnabas admonished the new converts in Antioch, Pisidia: "**Now when the congregation has broken up, many of the Jews and devout proselytes followed Paul and Barnabas, who, speaking to them persuaded them to continue in the grace of God**" (Acts 13: 43). Those who continue in grace will be divinely helped to discontinue with sin. To continue in grace is the secret of increasingly growing in the grace of God and experiencing the privileges of abundant grace.

b. Continue in Prayer

Prayer is the power base of a successful Christian life. The maxim – No prayer, no power is apt. Paul in most of his epistles, emphasizes the need for Christians to pray: For example, in Romans 12: 12, he enjoins believers to "**rejoice in hope, patient in tribulation, continuing steadfastly in prayer**". In Ephesian 6: 18, he wrote: "**Praying with all prayer and supplication in the spirit, being watchful to this end with all perseverance and supplication for all the saints**". Writing to the Colossian church on Christian grace he enjoined the Church "**to continue earnestly in prayer being vigilant in it with thanksgiving**" and urged the Church to pray for his team of missionaries (Col. 4: 2-3).

Believers are also enjoined to pray always and "**pray without ceasing**" (I Thess. 5: 17). Since we do not know when the end would come – the second coming of Christ – Jesus instructed believers on how to prepare for the future in other to endure. "**Watch** therefore for you do not know what hour your Lord is coming. But know this, if the master of the house had known what hour the thief would come, he would have watched and not allowed his house to be broken into" (Matt. 24: 42-43). The importance of watching and praying always was emphasized by Jesus in Luke 21: 36: "Watch therefore, and pray always that you may be counted worthy to escape all these things that will come to pass and to stand before the Son of Man". A Christian who is not watching and praying always will soon enter into temptation like Peter and his two colleagues who were sleeping when they should be praying and watching with Jesus(Matt. 26: 41).

c. Continue in the Word of God
The word of God contains all His plans and promises for His children. The entrance of His word into our hearts brings light which removes ignorance. The word of God encourages and motivates us in times of challenges. The word of God contains the truth that can set us free from any bondage or oppression of the devil. Jesus said: **"If you abide in my word, you are my disciple indeed"** (John 8: 31). In other words, the mark of true discipleship is ability to abide in the word of God.

d. Continue in sound doctrine
Jesus said: **"Whosoever wants to do my will must know about my doctrine"** (John 7: 17) – the undiluted teachings of Christ.

We have been warned against false teachers who will emerge in end time to teach false doctrines in order to pervert the hearts of believers.

Paul warned Timothy to take heed to his ministry and **"to himself and to the doctrine, continue in them, for in doing this, you will save both yourself and those who hear you"** (I Tim. 4: 16).

For Christians to grow in grace they must stand on solid ground doctrinally so that they will not be tossed to and fro like chaff on the sea. We should be careful about things we learn and through whom we learn them just as Paul warned Timothy in 2 Timothy 3: 14: **"But you must continue in the things which you have learned and been assured of, knowing from whom you have learned them"**. We must follow the example of the first church who **"continued in the doctrines of the apostles"** (Acts. 2: 42).

e. Continue in the Faith

For all converts into Christian faith, it is mandatory to continue in our new found faith, for us to reap the benefits of works of grace and in order to grow continually in faith. Strengthening the new converts in Lystra following their persecution and rejection from the city, Paul exhorted them **"to continue in faith, and saying, we must through many tribulations enter the kingdom of God"** (Acts 14: 22).

The phrase "the faith" signifies "the Christian faith," the faith which we all share in common; that is, "the common faith" (Tit. 1: 4), "the faith which was once delivered to the saints" (Jude vs. 3), which Paul kept (2 Tim. 4: 7) and which many shall "depart from" in these last days (I Tim. 4: 1). To continue in the faith also means to stand firm in the faith (I Cor. 16: 13), to be established in the faith (Col. 2: 7) and to continue believing God (Col. 1:23). Abraham believed God consistently even when his condition seemed hopeless. He never wavered in believing God's promise; in fact, his faith grew stronger and increased (Rom. 4: 19-21).

f. Continue in holiness

One of the principal pillars that can make us grow in faith is holiness. Without holiness no one can see God. In fact, we are saved so that we may serve in holiness and righteousness all the days of our life (Luke 1: 75). Living in holiness turns curse to blessing, for example, the first woman was cursed – sorrow through child labour in Gen. 3: 16, but the curse has been reversed; the believing woman will be saved if she continues in faith, in holiness and in modesty. "**Nevertheless she will be saved in child bearing if they continue in faith, love and holiness with self control**" (I Tim. 2: 15).

This passage (I Tim. 2: 15) directly relates to physical deliverance – deliverance from pain in childbearing. The same condition applies to spiritual salvation from sin and its consequences. Christians can be "saved" through trusting God and obeying His word. The sin of Adam brought divine "curse" on the human race; pain in child bearing is part of the curse (Gen. 3: 16). The salvation provided through Christ covers sin and its consequences – physical, material and spiritual. Therefore, through the grace of God, we have been saved from the "curse" of sin inherited from Adam (Gal. 3: 13).

g. Continue to trust in God's goodness

In Romans chapter eleven, Paul traced the history of Israel and their rejection of Jesus while clinging to Judaism at the expense of Christianity. The Gentiles embraced Christianity and all the blessings of works of grace to the chagrin of the Jews. But Paul was quick to remind the Gentiles that Israel's rejection is not final; in (Romans 11: 22) he said: "**Therefore consider the goodness and severity of God on those who fell, severity; but toward you, goodness, if you continue in His goodness. Otherwise you also will be cut off**". For the Gentiles to continue to be acceptable to God they must continue to trust in His goodness, otherwise they too will be cut off like the Judaizers because God is not a respecter of persons.

h. Endure to the end
Christian life is not a bed of roses. There are periods of tests and temptations, thick and thin, persecutions, triumphs and setbacks. It takes determination, commitment and perseverance to meet these challenges with equal mind.

Jesus told the disciples and, by extension, all believers. "**And you will be hated by all for my name's sake. But he who endures to the end will be saved**" (Matt. 10: 22). There is need for us to endure and sometimes we may need to give up our rights and benefits to please others as a sacrifice for peace and good neighbourliness. Jesus gave us an insight into lawlessness and other evils of the end of the age in Matt 24 and concluded that only "**those who endure to the end shall be saved**" (Matt. 24: 13).

i. Be a good Steward of Divine Grace
As beneficiaries of divine grace of salvation and the works of grace which include gifts of Holy Spirit, we have become God's stewards – caretakers, custodians and overseers. We are accountable to God how we use His gifts for the benefit of the

church. Peter wrote: "**As every man hath received the gift, even so minister the same one to another, as good stewards of the manifold grace of God**" (I Pet. 4: 10 KJV). Good stewardship requires faithfulness; this is an essential requirement (I Cor. 4: 1)

J. Abide in Christ

To abide in Christ means to remain in Him, to obey and to endure with Him. We must abide in Him and allow His word to abide in us. Jesus is the tree and Christians are the branches and for us to bear fruits as branches we must abide in (remain part of) the tree (John 15: 1-2).

Jesus said: "**Abide in Me, and I in you. As the branch cannot bear fruit of itself, unless it abides in the vine, neither can you, unless you abide in Me. I am the vine, you are the branches. He who abides in Me, and I in Him, bears much fruit; for without Me you can do nothing**" (John 15: 4-5).

Abiding in Christ is not only necessary for answer to prayer (John 15: 7), it also provides spiritual covering, protection and security. Moreover, constant abiding in Christ is necessary for our eternal salvation.

God provided "salvation" for the children of Israel in the land of Goshen, in Egypt – through the blood of animal. Each house must have blood as a sign, on the door posts. The blood provided covering, safety, security, and protection. However, their "salvation" was conditional; they must stay in their tents, no one must be out, while the death angel passed through the land. Anyone who "disobeyed" would not be "covered" or protected.

Then Moses called for all the elders of Israel and said to them: pick out and take lambs for yourselves according to your families, and kill the Passover lamb. And you shall take a bunch of hyssop, dip it in the blood that is in the basin, and strike the lintel and the two doorposts with the blood that is in the basin. And none of you shall go out of the door of his house until morning. For the Lord will pass through to strike the Egyptians, and when He sees the blood on the lintel and on the two doorposts, the Lord will pass over the door and not allow the destroyer to come into your houses to strike you. Exodus 12: 21-23.

Paul's voyage to Rome – a type of Christian experience and journey to heaven – is instructive and relevant. In the midst of wind of typhoon that threatened the lives of Paul and his fellow travelers, an angel assured him that no soul will be lost, except the ship (Acts 27:22). But this promise of salvation seemed to be conditioned: they will die unless they stayed on aboard.

Paul said to the centurion and the soldiers, "unless these men stay in the ship, you cannot be saved" (Acts 27:31).

Our ultimate salvation depends on abiding in Christ and continuing in grace. The blessings of grace can be forfeited, "except we abide in Christ."

Abide in His doctrine - Anyone not having God which results from abiding not in His doctrine does not belong to Him. He who commits sin is of the devil, he does not abide in His doctrine.

John writes: "**Whoever transgresses and does not abide in the doctrine of Christ does not have God. He who abides in the doctrine of Christ has both the Father and the Son**" (2 John vs. 9).

Abide in His Word - Christians are enjoined to allow the word of God to dwell in them richly (Col. 3;16). The word of God is the only truth that can set sinners free.

John counsels: "**Therefore let that abide in you which you heard from the beginning. If what you heard from the beginning abides in you, you will always abide in the Son and in the Father**" (I John 2: 24).

Abide in His fellowship - One of the works of grace is that after we are saved from sin we have fellowship with Christ. So in this fellowship, His anointing abides in us; we do not need a teacher because we have the Holy Spirit as our teacher. He teaches us the truth and in that teaching we must abide. He who abides in Him does not commit sin as sin separates people from God. John writes: "**But the anointing which you have received from Him abides in you, and you do not need that anyone teach you; but as the same anointing teaches you concerning all things, and is true, and is not a lie, and just as it has taught you, you will abide in Him. And now, little children, abide in Him that when He appears, we may have confidence and not be ashamed before Him at His coming**" (I John 2: 27-28).

Again, he said: **"When He shall appear, we shall be like Him; for we shall see Him as He is, because we shall fellowship with Him"** (I John 3: 2).

k. Practice the Teachings of Grace
Christians are trained by saving grace to be holy and live our lives to please the Lord regardless of any situation we find ourselves. For us to please God we must imbibe the teachings of grace and put to practice what we have learned. Paul, in his epistle to Titus, wrote:

"For the grace of God that brings salvation has appeared to all men, teaching us that, denying ungodliness and worldly lusts, we should live soberly, righteously and godly in the present age, looking for the blessed hope and glorious appearing of our great God and Saviour Jesus Christ".
(Titus 2: 11-13)

We should remember that it is not the hearers that are blessed but the doers of the word (Jam. 1: 22-23).

l. Humble yourself before God
The work of grace – salvation - opens our eyes to see how filthy and unworthy we are before God; that we are saved only by His mercy. This calls for total surrender and humility as clay in hand of the Lord who is the Potter. When we humble ourselves before Him, **"He gives us more grace because He resists the proud but gives grace to the humble"** (Jam. 4: 6). As Christian believers, we

should submit to God and resist the devil (I Pet. 5: 5-6).

m. Be strong in the Grace of God
We can only receive strength in the grace of God because by separating ourselves from Him we can do nothing.

Paul exhorted Timothy, his spiritual son: "**You therefore, my son, be strong in the grace that is in Christ Jesus**" (2 Timothy 2: 1). The more we show our commitment and loyalty to God, the more we become beneficiaries of His works of grace and the stronger we become.

n. Stand on the Grace of God
The grace of God is sufficient for all Christian believers in every situation and challenges that may confront us. We do not need to seek protection, assistance or support from any other source than to stand on God's grace. The Lord told Paul: "**My grace is sufficient for you**".

Writing to the Roman church on the fact that faith triumphs in trouble, Paul said: "**Jesus Christ through whom also we have access by faith into this grace in which we stand and, rejoice in hope of the glory of God**" (Rom. 5: 2).

o. Grow in Grace
As Christians, who have been saved by grace, we should remain faithful and loyal to Him who has saved us and brought us from darkness into His marvelous light. He who has begun the good works in us will help us to grow in grace and perfect His works in us.

Peter exhorts the church: "**to grow in the grace and knowledge of our Lord and Saviour Jesus Christ**" (2 Pet. 3: 18). This must be our desire always, to increasingly grow in grace. Thus, we can experience the privileges of abundant grace.

CHAPTER 11

GROWING IN GRACE

What is Growth?

Growth means increase, development, expansion, extension. Growth in grace therefore, signifies that as Christians we should be progressively becoming more Christ-like day by day. We must make ourselves available to God so that we can become usable, prepared vessels who are ready for His use. We must yield our lives to God and let Him work out the plan He has for our lives. "For we are Gods workmanship, created in Christ Jesus for good works, which God prepared beforehand that we should walk in them" (Eph. 2:10). There is absolute necessity for us to grow in grace and knowledge of our Lord Jesus Christ (2 Pet. 3:18).

Growing in Grace is our duty

On God's part, grace is given freely, but we have a responsibility to protect and develop it. God expects this sacred responsibility from every one entrusted with His grace or blessing.

But he who did not know, yet committed things deserving of stripes, shall be beaten with few. For everyone to whom much is given, from him much will be required; to whom much has been committed, of him they will ask the more.
(Luke 12:48)

Every blessing we receive from God – spiritual gifts, ministry talents, anointing, grace, etc – needs to be cultivated.

The parable of the talent (Matt. 25:14-30) aptly illustrates the point that all Christians are given equal opportunity according to their abilities to exercise their talents, gifts, anointing. What you do with your gifts/talents is entirely your choice and attitude. Growth will be natural, and effective when we exercise our gifts because growth is not forced on anyone.

Paul admonished Timothy: "to stir up the gift of God which is in you through the laying of hands" (2 Tim. 1:6). In 1 Timothy 4:14, Paul exhorted Timothy "not to neglect the gift that is in you which was given to you by prophecy and by laying of hands of the eldership." You grow in grace as you stir up the gift of God bestowed on you.

We are specifically commanded in the Word of God to "grow in grace" (2 Peter 3:18 KJV). The Greek word used here for "grow" is "auxano", which denotes to enlarge, to increase, to grow or to grow up. It is translated "increase" in John 3:30; 1 Cor. 3:6-7; Acts 6:7; 2 Cor. 9:10; 10:15.

Apostle Peter used the same word in 1 Peter 2:2, where he said:

Therefore, laying aside all malice, all deceit, hypocrisy, envy, and all evil speaking, as new born babes, desire the pure milk of the Word, that you may grow thereby.

The Bible has also used other related words to indicate growth or increase in grace. These include:

a. Abundance of Grace or Abundant Grace
This is rich, full and overflowing grace bestowed by Jesus to sinners by paying the supreme price that they may be saved from sin, and thus pass from condemnation to life (Rom. 5:17). The grace is greater on account of the thanksgiving of the greater number of those who have benefited from the abundant grace to the glory of God (2 Cor. 4:15).

b. Grace multiplied
We are being reminded by Peter in 2 Peter 1:2 that it is only through God the Father and the knowledge of His Son Jesus Christ that grace and peace can be multiplied unto us.

c. More Grace
This is the grace that is more than enough that God bestows on the humble that enables him to succeed and manifest the works of grace (James 4:6).

d. Greater Grace
In Acts 4:33, we are told that the apostles preached the doctrine of resurrection with great vigour, spirit, and courage. God Himself through them bore witness too, and His beauty shone, upon all their performances. Great Grace was upon all the apostles and believers. Christ poured out abundance of grace upon them and endued them with great power. More commitment to God's work commands more divine power which provokes greater grace.

e. Exceeding Grace
Paul talks about the exceeding grace in 2 Cor. 9:14, which is the extraordinary and enormous grace we receive in return for our liberal giving through the prayers of the beneficiaries of our gifts. Every sacrifice you make, by being a channel of blessings

to others, will always attract excessive grace from the Lord.

f. More Abundant Grace
There is "more abundant grace" to take care and cover our sins and weaknesses (Rom. 5:20). This is to magnify the riches of love of Christ and for the comfort and encouragement of believers who might consider the wound of Adam's sin or the gravity of their own sins, might begin to despair of a proportional remedy. Where there is guilt and wrath, He is ready with more grace and love to save upon an imputed righteousness than to condemn upon an imputed guilt.

How to Grow in Grace

Generally, we grow spiritually by making judicious, positive and purposeful use of the means of grace provided by God through His Word. While a child is born – not by himself, but by his parents – the child must determine to grow to become an adult. Grace has been given by God, but we need to determine to make it grow, to develop in grace and to "increase" in grace. It is God who gives the "increase", but we must "plant and water" to see increase (1 Cor. 3:6-7).

The means of growth in grace include the following:

a. A Consistent Prayer Life
Greater grace is received through prayer. The apostles were empowered with greater grace after a powerful mountain crushing prayer. Abundant grace was poured upon them as a confirmation of answer to their prayer (Acts 4:31-33).

Pray always for more grace – In the parable of the persistent widow, in Luke 18, Jesus underscores the importance of importunity of prayer for all believers. He also enjoins all believers "to watch and pray always that we may be counted worthy to escape all these things that will come to pass." In addition, to overcome trials, temptation and the wiles of the devil, we have to pray always (1 Thess. 5:17; Rom. 12:12).

Ask for more grace and it will be given – Salvation through grace brings a new convert closer to Christ and as a son of God, he has the added advantage of asking, seeking and knocking for more grace. Jesus said: "Ask and it will be given to you; seek and you will find; knock, and it will be opened to you" (Matt. 7:7). God loves His children in such a way that they lack nothing. James says however, that if we do lack wisdom, we should ask God for it. The reasonable thing to do therefore, is to pray for wisdom when facing problems.

God was willing to give Solomon anything he named. God said to Solomon one night: "Ask what I shall give you" (1 Kings 3:5). Solomon displayed a good amount of wisdom by asking for more wisdom to lead the people of Israel. God did not only grant his request, but also gave him what he did not ask for – riches, honour, long-life and conquest. Therefore, if you need something, ask, and you shall be given.

b. Be diligent
God rewards, blesses and honours diligent Christians (Heb. 11:6). Diligence is the secret of growth in grace and in Christian life in general.

Solomon writes: "He who has slack hand becomes poor, but the hand of the diligent makes rich" (Prov. 10:4)." The soul of a lazy man desires and has nothing; but the soul of the diligent shall be made rich" (Prov. 13:4).

Comparing the diligent and the hasty, Solomon said, while the diligent's plan increases, that of the hasty comes to poverty (Prov. 21:5).

It is only the diligent that will stand before kings and not before mean men (Prov. 22:29). Biblical examples, such as Joseph and Daniel, confirm the assertion of Solomon.

Through diligence we develop in Christian graces, moving from one level of grace to the next level, in the "ladder" of perfection.

And beside this, giving all diligence, add to your faith virtue; and to virtue knowledge; and to knowledge temperance; and to temperance patience; and to patience godliness; and to godliness brotherly kindness; and to brotherly kindness charity. For if these things be in you, and abound, they make you that ye shall neither be barren nor unfruitful in the knowledge of our Lord Jesus Christ.
(2 Peter 1:5-8 KJV)

God works these graces through us, as we make positive efforts, through diligence. Let us note the different graces mentioned by Peter, in their order of progress.
-Faith
-Virtue
-Knowledge

-Temperance
-Patience
-Godliness
-Brotherly kindness
-Charity or Love

Peter seems to doubly emphasize the importance of diligence in 2 Peter 1:10 KJV.

Wherefore the rather, brethren, give diligence to make your calling and election sure; for if you do these things, ye shall never fall.

The Apostle Paul has admonished us to be diligent – not only to grow in grace – but to remain in grace. Thus, we may not fall from grace.

Looking diligently lest any man fail of the grace of God: lest any root of bitterness springing up trouble you, and thereby many be defiled.
                    (Hebrews 12:15JKV)

c. More grace is received through Humility

Humility is the only "insurance" against humiliation. Grace can be lost through pride, but gained through humility (James 4:6; 1 Peter 5:6).

To grow in grace and be honoured by God, you must humble yourself (Prov. 3:34). The way up is down, you must first "take root downward", before you can "bear fruit upward" (2 kings 19:30).

The grace of God will increase in your life, as you "decrease" before God. John the Baptist said: "He must increase, but I must decrease" (John 3:30).

d. Grow in the Word
We grow in grace as we grow in the knowledge and application of the Word.

As fertilizer helps crops to grow, so the Word of God helps a Christian to grow in grace. God impressed it upon Joshua to obey His word as delivered by Moses and to meditate on it as panacea to his success (Josh. 1:7-8). The Word of God is compass to Christians. When we obey the Word, we shall surely be blessed (Psa. 1:1-3).

Therefore, we must allow the Word of God to dwell in us richly (Col. 3:16). As milk is essential for the growth of children so is the Word of God for Christians to grow in grace (1 Peter 2:2).

The Word of God is also the Word of grace – the source of grace (Acts 20:32). Grace is released and increased where the Word increases (Acts 19:20). When the apostles gave more time to the Word, the work of God increased. The Church grew in grace and in power (See: Acts 6:2-4, 7).

e. Fellowship with other Christians
Fellowship is one of God's provisions for blessing and imparting His grace and power upon Christians. Fellowship, from the Greek word "koinonia", means partnership, communion or participation. In fellowship we "share things in common" in a spiritual atmosphere. The grace or blessings of others can be imparted to us, as we "share" fellowship with others. As "iron sharpens iron" (Prov. 27:17), so the grace in one believer "sharpens" the grace in another believer.

Firstly: Have fellowship with the Triune God: Father (1 John 1:3), Son (1 Cor. 1:9; Phil. 3:10; 1 John 1:6) and the Holy Spirit (Phil. 2:1).

Secondly: Have fellowship with other Christians. The first church continued steadfastly in the apostles' doctrine and fellowship, their fear fell upon every soul and they experienced signs and wonders (Acts 2:42-43). Christians as light of the world are enjoined to live soberly and righteously to maintain fellowship with Jesus (1 John 1:3, 7).

f. Grow in Faith
We receive divine blessings – including growth in grace – through faith. Without faith it is "impossible to please God" (Heb. 11:6). Those who ignore faith in divine grace can make "shipwreck" (1 Tim. 1:19).

Faith and grace work together in the redemptive plan of God. Grace is given freely by God, but we receive it by faith. Only by grace we can come boldly to the throne of mercy (Heb. 4:16) because none of us has any good works (Eph. 2:8).

When we humble ourselves, we receive more grace to grow in faith.

Faith and grace are linked together in the Word of God. Where there is faith, grace is given. Therefore, where faith increases, grace increases also. Thus, we can conclude that: growth in faith (2 Thess. 1:4), brings growth in grace (2 Pet. 3:18); to continue in faith (Acts 14:22; Col. 1:23; 1 Tim. 2:15) is to continue in grace (Acts 13:43; 1 Tim. 2:15); to be justified by faith (Rom. 5:1) is to be justified by grace (Rom. 3:24; Titus 3:7); to be established in faith (Acts 16:5) is to be established in grace (Heb.

13:9); as we abound in faith (2 Cor. 8:7), we must abound in grace also (2 Cor. 8:7) and to depart from faith (1 Tim. 4:1) is to fall from grace (Gal. 5:4; 1 Tim. 1:19).

g. Honour God at your level of Grace
God honours those who honour Him (1 Sam. 2:30). The honour we have for God, we must show forth in our praises and our possessions. We must honour Him not only with our bodies and spirits but with all our earthly possessions which are His (Prov. 3:9, 10). If what we have increase and become substantial, they still belong to Him, we should honour Him; for it is God who gives us the power, ability, skill and grace to get wealth (Deut. 8:18).

When riches increase, we tend to honour ourselves (Deut. 8:17) and set our hearts on it (Psa. 62:10), but the more God gives us the more we should honour Him. We make mistake when we think that giving will undo us and make us poor.

Your level of grace or gifting may be little, but if you appreciate what God has given you, your grace can be greatly increased (Job 8:7). Therefore, Do not despise your small blessings (Zech. 4:10).

Let us learn from the man with one talent in Matthew 25. He buried the only talent and lost out. He was condemned to the utter darkness and his talent was given to another.

h. Do not abuse the grace of God
The gospel is a word of grace sounding in our ears, we must comply with the offer of reconciliation. Grace is superior to law and works, the grace of God freely given should be thankfully accepted (1 Cor.

1:4). We abuse the grace of God and make it ineffectual in our lives, when we ignore it (2 Cor. 6:1), treat it as meaningless (Gal. 2:21) or use it selfishly.

i. Be thankful for what you have
We are what we are by His grace. Whatever we have are divinely bestowed. We brought nothing to the world. We have to show our appreciation in praises and thanksgiving for His faithfulness (Psa. 100:1-4). In everything and in every situation, we should always show our appreciation (Col. 3:15; 1 Thess. 5:18).

j. Be faithful in little blessings
It is obvious that a person who is not faithful in little blessing cannot be faithful in a bigger thing (Luke 16:12). Christians are enjoined to be thankful. When the Samaritan came to thank Jesus after receiving his healing; Jesus asked: "Where are the nine others?" (Luke 17:17). This is a lesson to all of us to be thankful and faithful in little blessings – to God and our human benefactors.

CHAPTER 12

EVIDENCES OF GROWING IN GRACE

Growth is evident in every sphere of life – physical or spiritual. All living things, plants and human beings grow. There are forms of visible qualities which are reflected through a Christian who is growing in grace. Every Christian is designed to grow in Christ. Christians should grow progressively to become more Christ-like daily. Apart from physical process of growth, there are other elements of growth which are utterly important and which need to go along with physical growth. Growth in divine grace is noticeable, it can be seen, sensed, perceived and felt. Barnabas "saw" the evidence of the grace of God in the Christians in Antioch (Acts 11: 23). The senior apostles in Jerusalem "perceived" the grace of God in Paul and Barnabas and gave them "the right hand of fellowship" (Gal. 2: 9). In the spiritual realm, there is need to grow in character, capacity, understanding, relationships and in the following areas:

a. Increase in wisdom and spiritual stature

When a Christian grows in wisdom, he will increase in knowledge of the word of God and generally in understanding, learning and scholarship and consequently, these will enhance his spiritual stature.

At the age of 12years, Jesus stayed back in the temple while His parents had left for Nazareth, sitting in the midst of the teachers, listening and asking them questions and He amazed the scholars. The scripture testifies: **"And the child grew and became strong in spirit filled with wisdom; and the grace of God was upon Him"** (Luke 2: 40).

This is a testimony to the fact that Jesus grew physically, spiritually, emotionally and maturely as **"He increased in wisdom and stature and in favour with God and man"** (Luke 2: 52).

Acts 9:22 confirms that "Paul increased all the more in strength and confounded the Jews shortly after his conversion when he preached Christ in the synagogues". He had been equipped with wisdom and knowledge by the Holy Spirit to preach Christ as opposed to his former stand for Judaism and law which profits nothing.

b. Graceful utterances
The utterances of an immature person proceeds from arrogant mind or self-confidence but graceful utterance is Holy Spirit inspired, and proceeds from a mature being, the hall mark of humility and growth. For the same reason Christians are enjoined: **"Let your speech always be with grace, seasoned with salt, that you may know how you ought to answer each one"** (Col. 4: 6). As Christians we need to pray for the gift of wisdom so that our mouth would always be filled with gracious words (Eccl. 10: 12).

c. Submission to God's will in trials
It is easier to gauge the level of maturity of a Christian during trials. An immature Christian looks for a scape goat for his challenges, blames everyone including God for his predicaments. He gets discouraged and wants to give up. Job is a good example of a man who submitted to God's will during his trials. He maintained his absolute faith in God and he turned down the advice of his wife that he should deny God (Job 1: 20-20).

Paul had a lot of revelations of heaven but also some oppositions to keep him humble. God gave him the grace and power to overcome the thorn but, did not take it away. Paul took pleasure in his trials rather than discouragement (2 Cor. 12: 8-10).

d. Enduring power in rough times
According to the man of God, Robert Schullar, during tough times, the tough gets going because, according to him, "tough time never lasts but tough people do."

What a Christian needs most during rough and tough times is perseverance and indomitable spirit; a tenacious, never giving up spirit, the stillness of heart in tough times. When Paul was passing through rough times he encouraged himself: "**Therefore I take pleasure in infirmities, in reproaches, in needs, in persecutions, in distresses, for Christ's sake for when I am weak, then I am strong**" (2 Cor. 12: 10).

e. God's strength is reflected in weakness
God's power comes to play more in the weakness of a Christian in order to prove Himself strong. In our inabilities God manifests His ability and power to demonstrate He is on our side to turn our weakness to strength.

God told Paul, "My grace is sufficient for you, for my strength is made perfect in weakness" (2 Cor. 12:9). At the Red Sea, when the children of Israel became helpless while the Egyptian army pressed hard on them, God proved Himself strong by taking over their battle. He made a way for them in the Red Sea, threw the Egyptians into utter darkness and they all perished in the sea (Exd. 14: 24-28).

f. Grace in serving God

Salvation bestows unrestricted privilege and access to serve God in truth and spirit. But we have to be careful and watchful against pitfalls and temptation so that we do not fall from grace. Afflictions, persecutions and allurements to sin can make the Christian weak and his knees grow feeble, to dispirit and discourage him but this he must strive against and resist the devil with Holy Spirit power (Jam. 4: 6).

When a Christian overcomes these hindrances he will be in a better position to run his spiritual race with faith, patience and holy courage which will enable him walk more steadily and prevent him from wavering and wandering. Having overcome these obstacles he will be able to encourage other weaker Christians. As we receive the grace to serve God in holiness, we will be on top of our Christian race without being defiled like others who have become victims of the grand deception of the devil (Heb. 12: 15).

g. Strength in grace for battle

There is always ahead of Christians, our enemy the devil who is looking for whom to devour, hence we need to summon courage and be ready at all times to resist him. We can only do this successfully if we take advantage of the grace God has provided us.

Paul encouraged Timothy in 2 Timothy 2: 1 to be strong through God's grace and reminded him that God did not give him timidity, instead God equipped him with love, power and sound mind (2 Timothy 1: 7, 8). These are the works of grace deposited in us by the Holy Spirit. Love enables us to attract and connect with others, power gives us the courage and competence to get the job done while sound mind gives us the perspective and wisdom to grasp a vision and take the right steps.

When we are strong in the grace for battle, we would be able to constantly persevere in His work and overcome all challenges that may rise to distract our attention.

h. Divine ability for a higher level of ministry
As Paul rightly observed, as Christians, by God's grace we are what we are. It is the grace of God that enables us to work and by rewarding our efforts He ensures that we do not labour in vain. Paul worked so much with diligence and so much effort that he achieved tremendous success by divine grace. The more he laboured, the more productive he was, and the more humble he was in the opinion of himself, the more he appreciated the favour of God towards him. Paul wrote:

But by the grace of God I am what I am, and His grace toward me was not in vain; but I labour more abundantly than they all, yet not I, but the grace of God which was with me.
(1 Cor. 15: 10)

Paul, as pioneer leader of the Corinthian church, reminded the slow growing church, acting like babies that leadership development is a process not an event. Paul saw the church as a family, a field and a building (I Cor. 3: 1-23). He emphasized that the goal of a church as a building should be quality hence he saw himself as a master builder who had laid the foundation on which others built. But he was able to play this role successfully as a leader who reached higher level of the ministry because of the special grace bestowed upon him by the Lord (I Cor. 3: 10). It is the process of growth that grants us divine ability for a higher level of ministry.

i. Fruitful and effective ministry

Fruitful and effective ministry is a true manifestation of growing in grace. The purpose of God for choosing a believer to serve in His vineyard is to bear enduring fruit (John 15: 16). For us to be fruitful we must be lifelong learners – teachability begins with knowledge (Col. 1: 9), then results in application (Col. 1: 10).

Paul writes:

"That you may walk worthy of the Lord, fully pleasing Him, being fruitful in every good work and increasing in the knowledge of God".
(Col. 1: 10)

The psalmist enjoined believers to get their inward nourishment and refreshment from the word of God for fruitfulness, productivity, strength, durability and success. "He shall be like a tree planted by the rivers of water, that brings forth its fruit in its season, whose leaves also shall not wither; and whatever he does shall prosper" (Psalm 1: 3).

Similarly, when Joshua took over as successor of Moses, God charged him **"to be strong and courageous...this book of law shall not depart from your mouth, but you shall meditate in it day and night, that you may observe to do according to all that is written in it. For then you will make your way prosperous and then you will have good success**" (Joshua 1: 7, 8).

In Psalm 92: 12-14, the Psalmist wrote: "**The righteous shall flourish like a palm tree, he shall grow like a cedar in Lebanon. Those who are planted in the house of the Lord shall flourish in the courts of our God. They shall still bear fruit in old age; they shall be fresh and flourishing**".

Surely the secret of fruitful and effective ministry is in drawing from the nourishment of the word and living righteously through grace.

j. A life governed by humility
Humility is a visible quality that reflects in the life of a Christian as a hall mark of growing in grace.

According to Proverbs 3: 34, "**Surely He scorns the scorners but He gives grace to the lowly**". Those who exalt themselves shall certainly be abased. Those who scorn discipline, scorn to take God's yoke upon them, scorn to be beholden to His grace, who scoff at godliness and godly people, and take pleasure in bantering and exposing them, God will scorn them. In James 4: 6, we are taught to observe the difference God makes between pride and humility. God resists the proud but gives grace to the humble.

In John 3: 30, John the Baptist advanced the dignity of Christ and instructed his disciples concerning him that, instead of grieving that so many went to Jesus, he was not at all displeased that the effect of this was the diminishing of his own interest. John talked of Christ's increase and his own decrease, "He must increase but I must decrease". John was conscious of his calling and limitation, he was contented to advance the cause of Christ, and lived a life governed by humility. No wonder Jesus Christ said of John; "among those born of women there has not risen one greater than John the Baptist". (Matt. 11:11).

k. A consistent life of holiness
In the prophecy of Zacharias, Luke 1: 74, 75, it is manifestly clear that God delivered sinners from the bondage of sin so that they would be enabled "to serve God without fear." They are put in a holy safety that they may serve God in holy security and serenity of mind. God must be served in obedient fear, an awakening quickening fear as opposed to slavish fear like that of a slothful servant who sees his lord as a hard master.

In Heb. 12: 14-15, Paul enjoins Christians to walk patiently under affliction so that we can walk so quietly and peaceably towards men and God because faith and patience will enable us to follow peace and holiness too, as a man follows his calling. It is the duty of a Christian to follow peace with all men, even when he is in a suffering state. Peace and holiness are connected; there can be no true peace without holiness, hence it is mandatory for us to live a consistent life of holiness if we want to be at peace with God and men.

For us to live a life of consistent holiness we must be obedient to the Lord and consistently "cleanse ourselves from all filthiness of the flesh and spirit, perfecting holiness in the fear of God" (I Cor. 7: 1).

l. A consistent life of prayer
We grow by praying much, and the more we grow, the more we will love to pray. The parable of the

importunate widow in Luke 18: 1-8 is designed to teach us fervency in prayer. Christ spoke it with this intent, to teach us that "men ought always to pray and not faint" vs. 1. It supposes that all God's children are praying people. It is our honour, privilege and duty to pray and when we neglect it, it is sin (I Sam. 12: 23). We must pray, and never grow weary of praying. In I Timothy 2: 8, Paul advocates the raising of frontier men of prayer everywhere; "**that men pray everywhere**". We must pray in our closets, pray in our families, pray at meals and when we are on our journeys, pray in the private and in public gatherings. It is the will of God, too, that we should lift up holy hands – pure from the pollution of sin - because if we regard iniquity in our hearts, God will not hear us (Psalm 66: 18).

Paul admonished Christians to guard their attitudes and replace worry with prayer and to think on the positive things that edify (Phil. 4:6-7).

Christians weapon of war against the devil or any human opposition could be found only in prayers. Daniel triumphed over the conspiracy of the men who plotted his being thrown into lions den through the weapon of prayer (Dan. 6: 10). Epaphras, a co-labourer with Paul, though he was held in prison by persecutors, he used the weapon of prayer to uphold new converts "**that you may stand perfect and complete in the will of God**" (Col. 4: 12).

The apostles and the early church used the weapon of prayer to forge ahead despite persecutions, imprisonments and other depravations by the Jews and Gentiles. As they preached and prayed, God gave them the boldness, courage and confirmed His word with signs, wonders and miracles (Acts 4: 23-33).

Our Lord Jesus Christ was a man of prayer. He often left His disciples behind and went up to the mountain to pray. Even before He began His ministry, He went alone to pray for 40 days. He was able to overcome the devil's temptation through the power of prayer (Matt. 4: 1-10). As He began with prayer He ended with prayer in the garden of Gethsemane where He engaged in spiritual battle (Luke 22: 40-44). He faced the battle alone, He was totally in submission to God's will and received strength.

m. Giving gracefully and generously
Growing in grace is reflected in our giving. A growing Christian will give with simplicity (Rom. 12: 8), regularly (I Cor. 16:12), willingly (2 Cor. 8: 12), cheerfully (2 Cor. 9: 7) and bountifully (2 Cor. 9:6).

Paul encouraged generosity among the Corinthians by bragging on the poverty – stricken Macedonian church proving that liberality has nothing to do with feeling comfortable or having abundance (2 Cor. 8: 2).The Church in Macedonia excelled in giving, a good example to be followed by Christians. The early Church was a giving church, they had all things in common. **"There was no one among them that lacked; for all who were possessors of lands or houses sold them, and brought the proceeds of the things that were sold, and laid them at the apostles' feet and they distributed to each as anyone had need**" (Acts 4: 34-35).

Dorcas was a convert who lived in Joppa and embraced the faith of Christ. She was eminent above many others in works of charity, she showed her faith by her works of liberal giving. Among other good works, she was remarkable for her alms, works of piety and benevolence flowing from love to her neighbours. She was commended for the alms deed and her works of charity (Acts 9: 36-43). So as believers whatever our hands find we should do it to the best of our ability.

n. A growing passion for Christlikeness
As we grow as Christians, we must set out our priorities as Paul did in Phil. 3: 10-12. Paul communicated his priorities by setting aside all the gains of the past in order to gain Christ. What was paramount in his heart was to know Christ more, experience His power, share in and complete His sufferings and ultimately be conformed to His death (Phil. 3:10-11). He did all these for the purpose of attaining the resurrection. As a Christian you should get your priorities right and narrow the wedge of your focus to the essentials – passion for Christlikeness. As the apostle was focused on happiness of heaven – resurrection of the dead - this too should be our priority. This should be the ultimate goal and crowning glory of our faith. When we see Him, we shall be like Him, "**but we know that when He is revealed, we shall be like Him, for we shall see Him as is. And everyone who has this hope in Him purifies Himself, just as He is pure**" (I John 3: 2-3).

o. Divine favour
Where there is divine grace, there is favour. The grace of God bestows on us favour of God and men; and who God favours, men favour also. As we grow in grace, we should trust God to open greater doors of favour, in life and ministry.

Favour with God - Favour with God is that goodwill, acceptance and blessings which God shows to His children. Favour represents the position one enjoys with God when He is favourably disposed towards him. For example, Isaiah speaks of the day, year or time of divine favour – the day of the Lord when all the blessings of the covenant shall be released upon God's people (Isa. 49: 8; 58: 5; 61: 2).

Mary had favour with God when she was the chosen vessel for God's highest purposes. The angel said to her; "**Rejoice, highly favoured one, the Lord is with you; blessed are you among women...Do not be afraid, Mary, for you have found favour with God**" (Luke 1: 28, 30). Solomon reminds us that only good people (Children of God) can have favour with God. "**A good man obtains favour from the Lord, but a man of wicked intentions, He will condemn**" (Proverbs 12: 2).

Favour with men - If a man's way is pleasing and acceptable to God, he will have favour with men. Thus, Joseph was diligent and honest in the house of Potiphar, he found favour with his master and made him the overseer of his household (Gen. 39: 4). As a child of God, you must serve your employer or boss loyally, diligently and faithfully to enable you have favour with God and men. Even when Joseph was imprisoned for the offence he never committed, God made him to have favour with the keeper of the prison (Gen. 39: 21).

Esther had favour with God and programmed her to become queen and a channel of blessings to the Jews. She found favour with Hegai, the eunuch in charge of candidates competing for the queenship.

Consequently, she had favour with King Ahasuerus and she was crowned the queen (Esther 2: 15, 17).

The early church had favour with all the people because they continued to live by the teachings of the apostles, breaking of bread, praising God, they lived communal life and **"the Lord added to the church daily those who were being saved"** (Acts 2: 47).

Jesus advanced in wisdom and favour because He had favour with God and men (Luke 2: 52). Therefore the secret for success and breakthrough in life or ministry is to please God so that we can carry His favour and once we have favour with God, the favour with men becomes a common place.

Showing favour to others - Whatever a man sows, the same he shall reap. If a man sows mercy he shall receive mercy, the one who sows money by giving, shall receive money. A person who sows favour will surely receive favour from God and men. Conversely, a person who sows the wind shall reap the whirlwind.

We are exhorted by the Psalmist; **"A good man showeth favour, and lendeth: he will guide his affairs with discretion"** (Psalm 112: 5 KJV). He that does good and shows favour with his estate shall through the providence of God increase it by his prudence. **"He shall guide his affairs with discretion and his God instructs him to discretion and teaches him"** (Isa. 28:26). It is part of the character of a good man that he will use his discretion in managing his affairs, in getting and saving, that he may have to give. It is part of the promise to him who uses his discretion to show favour that God will give him more.

It is the happiness of "**a good man that he shall not be moved...the righteous shall be in everlasting remembrance (and the memorial of it) endures for ever**" (Psalm 112: 6-9).

p. Spiritual progress
Another discernible evidence of growing in grace is spiritual progress through the manifestation of works of grace. Job wrote: "**Yet the righteous will hold to his way, and he who has clean hands will be stronger and stronger**" (Job 17: 9). The righteous is the saint, he is an upright man, honest and sincere, that acts from a steady principle with a single eye. He will be made more vigorous and lively in his duty, more warm and affectionate, more resolute and undaunted. In order to enable him to grow in grace, he will not only hold on his way, but will grow stronger and stronger in grace, giftings and in spiritual, material and physical blessings.

Writing of the blessedness of dwelling in the house (presence) of God, the Psalmist said; "They go from strength to strength; each one appears before God in Zion" (Psalm 84: 7). In other words, those that press forward in their Christian course shall find God adding grace to their graces (John 1: 16). They shall be changed from glory to glory (2 Cor. 3: 18), from one degree of glorious grace to another, till, at length, "everyone of them that appears before God in Zion," will continue to grow stronger and give glory to Him and receive more blessings from Him. Those who grow in grace shall at last, be made perfect in glory. We must go from one duty to another, from prayer to the word, from practicing what we have learned to learn more, and if we do this, we shall still continue to make steady spiritual progress from our youth until our old age, we shall still bear fruit (Psalm 92:12, 14).

q. Effective use of gifts for Ministry
Spiritual gifts are given according to individual's ability (Matt. 25: 15), level of faith, calling for profiting (benefit of the church) I Cor. 12: 7) and according to the measure of Christ's gift (Ephes. 4: 7).

For every gift or ministry, there is a measure of grace to function effectively in that gifting. Thus, gift can be misused where grace is lacking, for example, Samson (Judg. 14: 6; 16: 1, 21) and Balaam (Num. 22: 28; 2 Pet. 2: 15, 16).

Every assignment requires an anointing. Anointing is the power God has provided us to remove a burden or destroy yoke of bondage existing on another (Isa. 6:1-4; 10:27). Specific assignments require specific anointing:

-A leadership anointing enables you to love
-An administrative anointing produces order
-A healing anointing releases health
-A psalmist anointing unlocks worship
-A wisdom anointing illuminates
-A prophet's anointing reveals the will of God.

As Christians, we all have a particular call or gifting which is ours through our heavenly Father's choice. Our calling by God to our work and service for Him, is an expression of the heart of God and carries with it the very hallmark of heaven. It is something to value and we should be concerned to work it out in the most effective way possible. We need constantly to polish this call or gifting of God and use it to its greatest potential for the good of others (2 Tim. 1: 6). We are saved by grace and called into grace. Grace is more than particular gifts of the Spirit. The gifting no doubt comes with the grace God has given us, but this grace is a deep and powerful reality in the lives of those who know it's their calling.

Every resource (gifts) God provides should be in use. Every believer is a steward of the abilities he or she has been given (Rom 12: 6). When we faithfully use our gifts, more graces shall be given to us (Matt. 25: 29). Anyone who fails to use his gift despises the Giver and His grace, and that gift will be taken away and given to others (Matt. 25: 28).

CHAPTER 13

THE EFFICACY OF GRACE

The grace of God is supernatural, it comes from God to humans. And as such, it is efficacious – it is sure to produce its desired effect or accomplish its purpose. The word "efficacy" simply means effectiveness, efficiency, usefulness, potency, productiveness, fruitfulness.

Therefore, by the efficacy of grace, we mean that Divine grace has the power and capability to fulfill God's purpose in human lives, to accomplish the effect desired by God in every believer and in every circumstance.

The efficacy of Divine grace can be based on the efficacy of His Word and of the atonement. The Word of God which we must believe to be saved is efficacious.

The Psalmist wrote:

The Works of His hands are verity and judgment; all His commandments are sure.
(Psalm 111:7 KJV)

Isaiah also wrote:

So shall My word be that goeth forth out of my mouth: it shall not return unto Me void, but it shall accomplish that which I please, and it shall prosper in the thing whereto I sent it.
(Isaiah 55:11 KJV)

According to David, all the commandments of God are "sure"-reliable, trustworthy or faithful in fulfilling its purpose. And, according to Isaiah, His Word will surely "accomplish" all God wants it to do and it will "prosper". The Hebrew word used in Isa. 55:11 for "accomplish" is "Asah" which denotes to do, to make, to accomplish, to bestow, to fulfill, to finish or to bring to pass, to perform.

The atonement is efficacious; the blood of Jesus has power to save, to heal and meet all needs.

In his admonition to praise the Lord, David said:

Who forgives all your iniquities, who heals all your diseases.
(Psalm 103:3)

Apostle John wrote:

But if we walk in the light as He is in the light, we have fellowship with one another, and the blood of Jesus Christ His Son cleanses us from all sin. If we say we have no sin, we deceive ourselves, and the truth is not in us. If we confess our sins, He is faithful and just to forgive us our sins and to cleanse us from all unrighteousness.
(1 John 1:7-9)

This is the true essence of "efficacy". If the Gospel of grace (Act 20:24) – the Word of God- which sinners must hear and believe – and the atonement which is the "price" for our redemption are efficacious, then the divine means by which salvation is received is also efficacious. So we may well say that "the grace of God which brings salvation" is efficacious. Its efficacy is established on the efficacy of the Word and the Atonement and, most importantly, on the sovereignty of the Giver of grace.

Moreover, it is worthy of note that grace is linked with the efficacy of the atonement.

Paul writes:

But we see Jesus, who was made a little lower than the angels, for the suffering of death crowned with glory and honour, that He, by the grace of God, might taste death for everyone. For it was fitting for Him, for whom are all things, in bringing many sons to glory, to make the captain of their salvation perfect through sufferings.
(Hebrews 2:9-10)

It was God's grace to us that led Christ to His death. If, therefore, the death of Christ is efficacious, then the grace that made the atonement possible and by which we receive the benefits of the atonement cannot be less efficacious; the grace of God is efficacious to bring into effect the divine purpose for the atonement.

Scriptural Basis for the Efficacy of Grace

In addition to the Scriptures above, there are some positive scriptural facts for this doctrine. These include:

a. **The Lord is able to save to the uttermost**
Wherefore he is able also to save them to the uttermost that come unto God by him, seeing he ever liveth to make intercession for them.
(Heb. 7:25 KJV)

The Greek word used here for "uttermost" is "Panteles", which denotes "full ended", complete, uttermost, entire. The saving grace is powerful, full and complete; it is powerful enough to save a soul to the last limit-from beginning to the end.

It is also by this grace that we are "kept saved", divinely kept from falling.

Now to Him who is able to keep you from stumbling. And to present you faultless. Before the presence of His glory with exceeding joy. To God our Saviour, Who alone is wise, Be glory and majesty; dominion and power, both now and forever. Amen.
(Jude 24, 25)

b.   Its effect is supernatural
Grace belongs to God, it is from God and it is given by God. It is called "the grace of God"- not the grace of man (see: Acts 11:23; 11:43; 1 Cor 3:10; 15:10 etc.). Therefore, it is capable of producing supernatural effects and fulfilling Divine purposes.

c.   Divine grace works efficaciously
Paul speaks of the effectual working power of grace in Eph. 3:7; he wrote:

Of which I became a minister according to the gift of the grace of God given to me by the effective working of His power.

The Greek word used here is "energeia", which denotes "efficiency", strong, effectual working. It is used in this verse of grace which is efficacious in its working.

The adjective "energes" is used in Hebrew 4:12 for "powerful". It describes the efficacy of the word of God.

For the word of God is alive and powerful. It is sharper than the sharpest two-edged sword, cutting between soul and spirit, between joint and marrow. It exposes our inner most thoughts and desires.
(Hebrews 4:12 NLT)

The verb form "energeo" is also used for the efficacy or the effectual working power of the word. The word means to be efficient, active, to make effectual.

For this reason we also thank God without ceasing, because when you received the word of God which you heard from us, you welcomed it not as the word of men, but as it is in truth, the word of God, which also effectively works in you who believe.
(1 Thessalonians 2:13)

d. The grace of God is sufficient to meet every need

This is clearly stated in 2 Cor. 12:9, where the Lord assured Paul. As humans, we are insufficient (2 Cor 2: 16; 3:5), deficient and incapable by our own strength (Zech 4:6). But God's grace is our sufficiency; the sufficiency of grace takes care of our insufficiencies and human infirmities.

Paul used the Greek word "arkeo" for "sufficient" here, which means to suffice, strong enough. The grace of God is "strong enough" to meet all human needs. It is strong enough to save and sanctify the believer; it is strong enough to sustain and strengthen us in our weaknesses (2 Cor. 12:10).

e. Grace can perfect all our imperfections

We are all imperfect beings; even the best saints still strive towards perfection.

Not that I have already attained, or am already perfected; but I press on, that I may lay hold of that for which Christ Jesus has also laid hold of me.
(Philippians 3:12)

But God can "perfect" our "imperfections" and strengthen our weaknesses, by the effectual working power of His grace.

David said:

The LORD will perfect that which concerneth me, thy mercy, O LORD endureth for ever: forsake not the works of thine own hands.
(Psalm 138:8 KJV)

His daily prayer for the church was for this purpose: to "perfect that which is lacking" in their faith. In answer to prayer, God releases the grace that makes imperfect beings to function as though they were "perfect".

f. Grace can finish what God has started in us

Divine grace is available to help us finish what God has started in us. Grace is strong enough to finish its saving work through us and in us.

Inasmuch that we desired Titus, that as he had begun, so he would also finish in you the same grace also.
(2 Corinthians 8:6 KJV)

Again, Paul wrote:

Being confident of this very thing, that He who has begun a good work in you will complete it until the day of Jesus Christ.
(Philippians. 1:6)

The Greek word used here for "perform" is "epiteteo", which denotes to fulfill, further, to completely accomplish.

The Lord Himself is the "Author and Finisher of our faith" (Heb. 12:2). He "finished" His work of redemption on the cross (John 17:4; 19:30). It was the divine grace in Him that enabled Him to finish His Divine assignment.

We are told that Jesus was "full of grace" (John 1:14); this was the power that helped Him to start and finish His Work. This same grace is available to us; we can fully finish God's work in our lives, through His grace.

g.   The grace is unlimited in its scope
The grace of God is unlimited in its operation, where sin, sinners and human needs are concerned.

i.)   Unlimited grace for sin
Grace is efficacious enough work in every sinner and fulfill God's purpose for their lives. No sin is too great to be touched by grace, no sinner is beyond

the reach of grace. Abundant grace is available for "abundant sin".

For if by one man's offence death reigned through the one, much more those who receive abundance of grace and of the gift of righteousness will reign in life through the One, (Jesus Christ) Therefore, as through one man's offence judgment came to all men, resulting in condemnation, even so through one Man's righteous act the free gift came to all men, resulting in justification of life. For as by one man's disobedience many were made sinners, so also by one Man's obedience many will be made righteous. Moreover the law entered that the offence might abound. But where sin abounded, grace abounded much more.
(Rom. 5:17-20)

Grace can lift the vilest sinner – prostitutes, drug addicts, criminals, etc- from the "gutter of sin", to the mountain of holiness.

ii.) Grace is unlimited by race, culture or gender - The Gospel is to be preached to every creature, in every nation.

The task of the Great Commission to preach the gospel of Jesus Christ is committed to all Christians, to preach and teach in all nations of the world, to give opportunity to all human race to hear good news that Jesus died for sinners and rose from the dead for their justification. "Go into all the world and preach the gospel to every creature. He who believes and is baptized shall be saved but he who does not believes will be condemned" (Mark 16:15-16).

There is no racial or cultural limitation in the efficacy of God's grace. The grace to be saved from sin is extended to all sinners irrespective of race, creed, culture, position or gender.

God is not a respecter of persons. He demonstrated this to the astonishment of Peter who was preaching to Cornelius, his family and friends who were non-Jews. Without laying of hand, they received the baptism of the Holy Spirit by speaking in tongue, when they heard the Word of God. Peter said; "In truth I perceive that God shows no partiality. But in every nation whoever fears Him and works righteousness is accepted by Him (Acts 10:34, 35).

We are sons and heirs. Paul wrote: "There is neither Jew nor Greek, there is neither slave nor free, there is neither male nor female, for you are all one in Christ" Gal. 3:28).

iii.) Its universality
Because Christ died to save "all men" (Heb 2:9), He is the Saviour of "all men" (1 Tim. 4:10), and God wants "all men to be saved" (1 Tim 2:4), the grace of God that brings salvation is extended to "all men"- that is all humans. Writing to Titus, Apostle Paul said; "For the grace of God that brings salvation has appeared to all men" (Titus 2:11).

h. The transforming power of grace
The efficacy is grace is evident in its power to transform lives. Lives that would have been "condemned" or "written off" have been supernaturally transformed through the mediation of Divine grace.

The following are examples:

i. The woman at the well

She was a woman of unsavoury reputation. This woman who at different times had lived with six different men as husband was at the well to draw water when Jesus met her. Through their discussion Jesus told her of her unsavoury reputation and disclosed to her that He was the Messiah spoken about in the scripture (John 4:17-19, 26).

She became an evangelist. The woman abandoned her water pot and ran to the city to announce that she had seen the Messiah. Everyone in the city trooped out to the well to have a glance at Jesus. He preached to them. They eventually urged Jesus to stay with them for two days to hear more of the word of the Kingdom (John 4:28-30, 40).

"And many of the Samaritans of that city believed Him because of the word of the woman who testified; "He told me all that I ever did" (John 4:39).

ii. Saul of Tarsus

Saul was a blood thirty persecutor.

Before he was saved, Saul persecuted the church and caused many disciples to be imprisoned. He took active part in the killing of Stephen, the first martyr (Acts 8:1-2).

Having received letter of authority to arrest and bring for prosecution disciples at Damascus, God met him on the way and he gave his life to Jesus (Acts 9:1-9).

He became a tender hearted preacher of the Gospel. After his conversion, he preached Christ in the synagogues that Jesus is the Son of God (Acts 9:20). Concerning Paul the scripture testified: "But Saul increased all the more in strength, and confounded the Jews who dwelt in Damascus, proving that this Jesus is the Christ" (Acts 9:22). He later joined the church in Antioch where the Holy Spirit chose him and Barnabas as missionaries to the Gentiles where they established many churches. He appeared before Governor Felix (Acts 24:10-21), King Agrippa and Festus (Acts 25: 12-26). He used the opportunity to preach the gospel of Jesus to them before he appealed to Caesar. He wrote half of the New testament books, a victim of persecution, shipwrecks, beaten many times by the Jews but remained a loyal solder of Christ who died at his post (2 Timo. 4:6-8).

iii.   The cold hearted jailer
Before his encounter with saving grace: In Philippi, Paul and Silas were beaten and their cloths torn by the magistrate before he delivered them to the jailer who treated them as common criminals, "he put them into the inner prison and fastened their feet in the stacks" (Acts 16:23-24).

After conversion he became gentle, sympathetic and humble. While in prison, Paul and Silas were not despondent, they sang and praised the Lord in the night and miraculously, all the doors of the prison were opened and their chains fell from their legs. The Jailer thought Paul and Silas had escaped, so he wanted to kill himself, but Paul assured him they were still in custody.

The jailor was surprised and realized that they were true men of God. He asked how he could be saved and took the men to his house, treated their wound and all his household believed. He became a changed person, humble and accorded them with courtesy (Acts 16:30-34).

I.   Divine grace is efficacious beyond this age
The efficacy of Divine grace is not limited to this Church Age- the Dispensation of Grace. The grace that brings salvation through faith, in this present Age, will yet work effectually in the hearts of the believers in Jesus in the post-Rapture Era. At present, the Jews –the Lord's ancient people- are "partially blind" because of their unbelief. They will remain "spiritually blind" in this state of unbelief and rejection of Christ, until "the fullness of the Gentles".

Paul wrote:

For I do not desire, brethren, that you should be ignorant of this mystery, lest you should be wise in your own opinion, that blindness in part has happened to Israel until the fullness of the Gentiles has come in.
(Rom. 11:25)

Their rejection of God's saving grace has opened the door of salvation to the Gentiles. According to Paul, Israel's rejection is not final.
I say then, have they stumbled that they should fall? Certainly not! But through their fall, to provoke them to jealousy, salvation has come to the Gentiles. Now if their fall is riches for the world, and their failure riches for the Gentiles, how much more their fullness.
(Rom. 11:11-12)

According to Paul, their unbelief is a blessing for the Gentiles; it has opened the door to salvation for "as many that receive" Jesus Christ. "But as many that receive Him are given Power to become children of God, Who are born, not of blood nor the will of flesh nor the will of man, but of God" (John 1:11-12).

However, God will yet again remember the Jews and have mercy on them. They, too, will be saved at the appropriate time.

Paul also wrote:

And so all Israel will be saved, as it is written: There shall come out of Zion, the Deliverer, and He will turn away ungodliness from Jacob; For this is My covenant with them; when I take away their sins.
(Rom. 11:26-27)

At the Second Advent, just at the end of the Great Tribulation, "all eyes" – including the Jews- will see Jesus Christ. (Rev. 1:7).

The same Spirit of grace that is available to us (Heb. 10:29), that wrought salvation in our hearts, will be divinely poured out upon them. The Spirit of grace will convict them of their sin; and they will repent and mourn. Consequently, they will be forgiven, restored and reconciled back to God.

God, speaking through Zechariah in Zech. 12:10-14, said:

And I will pour on the house of David and on the inhabitants of Jerusalem the Spirit of grace

and supplication; then they will look on Me whom they pierced. Yes, they will mourn for Him as one mourns for his only son, and grieve for Him as one grieves for a firstborn. "In that day there shall be a great mourning in Jerusalem, like the mourning at Hadad Rimmon in the plain of Megiddo. And the land shall mourn, every family by itself: the family of the house of David by itself, and their wives by themselves; the family of the house of Nathan by itself, and their wives by themselves, the family of house of Levi by itself, and their wives by themselves; the family of Shimei by itself, and their wives by themselves; all the families that remain, every family by itself, and their wives by themselves.

BIBLIOGRAPHY

1. Bancroft, Emery, Christian Theology, Michigan: Zondervan Publishing House, 1976.

2. Bere, C. Michael, Bible Doctrine for Today, Florida: Pensacola Christian College, 1988.

3. Bounds, E. M., The Essentials of Prayer, Chicago: Moody Press, 1980.

4. Coles, Elisha, God's Sovereignty, Michigan: Baker Book House, 1979.

5. Guthrie, Donald, The Pastoral Epistles, Leicester: Inter-versity Press, 1999.

6. Henry, Mathew, Mathew Henry's Commentary On The Whole Bible, London: Marshall Pickering, 1960.

7. Hurding, Roger, Pathway to Wholeness, Pastorial Care in a Postmodern Age, London: Holder and Stoughton, 1998.

8. Nee, Watchman, The King and The Kingdom of Heaven, New York: Christian Fellowship Publishers, Inc, 1978.

9. Newton, John (1725-1805), Amazing Grace, United Methodist Hymnal, USA: The United Methodist Publisher, 1989.

10. Ryan, Cliton, Jesus Christ Speaks From The Mountain, Birmingham: European Theological Seminary, 2000.

11. Strong, James, The New Strong's Exhaustive Concordance of The Bible, Nashville: Thomas Nelson Publishers, 2010.

12. Schuller, Robert, Tough Times Never Last, But Tough People Do, Ibadan, Nigeria: Reprinted by permission, by Scripture Union, 1997.

13. Tasker, R.V.G., The Gospel According to St. John, Michigan: William B. Eerdmans Publishing Company, 1978.

14. The New Encyclopedia of Christian Quotations, Hamshire: John Hunt Publishing Inc; 2000.

15. The Concise English Dictionary, London: Oxford University Press, 1961.

16. Vine, W.E., Vine's Expository Dictionary of New Testament Words, Massachusetts: Hendrickson Publishers, (no date).

17. Zondervan Pictorial Bible Dictionary, Michigan: Zondervan Publishing House, 1967.

www.ingramcontent.com/pod-product-compliance
Lightning Source LLC
LaVergne TN
LVHW051117080426
835510LV00018B/2080